BIZARRE HISTORY

BIZARRE HISTORY

Strange Happenings, Stupid Misconceptions, Distorted Facts and Uncommon Events

JOE RHATIGAN

imagine!
Publishing

An Imagine Book
Published by Charlesbridge
85 Main Street, Watertown, MA 02472
(617) 926-0329
www.charlesbridge.com

Printed in China, May 2013.

Library of Congress Cataloging-in-Publication Data Available

ISBN 978-1-62354-034-0 (Special Edition for Barnes & Noble)

2 4 6 8 10 9 7 5 3 1

For information about custom editions, special sales,
premium and corporate purchases, please contact
Charlesbridge Publishing at specialsales@charlesbridge.com

CONTENTS

VILLAGE IDIOTS AND FOUNDERING FATHERS

Whenever I contemplate history, I imagine a dusty old guy with whiskers, a pipe, and a long, boring story that I'm going to be forced to listen to . . . and memorize. In fact, before I started this book, I had little idea of the depth and breadth of history's personality. History, you see, is actually a scandalous gossip and a born liar, prone to hyperbole and drunken outbursts. History parties hard and says rude things to the neighbors. Perhaps most of all, history is weird, bizarre, and (once you get rid of all the parts that you're only supposed to know because "it's good for you") fascinating!

Think of this book as history's unauthorized biography (preferably by Kitty Kelley)—all the juicy bits without the historical relevance getting in the way of a good time. I mean, it's all well and good that the Founding Fathers founded whatever it is they founded; however, it's tremendous fun reading about how they foundered! Or what about the first balloon flight? It was a truly poignant moment in humankind's history (blah, blah, blah), but what's really cool is what happened when the cameras stopped rolling (I know, no cameras back then, but work with me here): The balloon landed miles away in a small village, and the locals, thinking they were being attacked by an airborne monster, tore it to pieces, tied it to the tail of a horse, and paraded the conquered

beast up and down the road. Now *that's* history one can get excited about! Why? Not because those villagers were idiots (no matter what I call them), but because this totally awesome tidbit doesn't usually make it into the footnotes of history textbooks. And that's too bad, because those villagers' actions tell us just as much about eighteenth century France as the actual balloon launch.

The stories I selected for *Bizarre History* don't attempt to make sense of the past, but they do show us how far we've come and the long journey we have yet before us.

Just kidding!

But seriously, we can learn from history—even this drunken stepchild of history that revels in our foolish behavior over the thousands of years in which we've been taking notes as well as in the silly things we believe to be true today.

THOUGHTS ABOUT HISTORY
(FROM PEOPLE SMARTER THAN ME)

In William Dean Howells's book *My Mark Twain*, he recounts a conversation with Twain about history. Howells said, "I wonder why we hate the past so." Twain responded, "It's so damned humiliating."

"The very ink with which all history is written is merely fluid prejudice."—Mark Twain

"That generations of historians have resorted to what might be called 'proof by haphazard quotation' does not make the procedure valid or reliable; it only makes it traditional."—Lee Benson, social historian

"History is a myth that men agree to believe."—Napoleon Bonaparte

"History is the distillation of rumour."—Thomas Carlyle, nineteenth-century Scottish writer

"I don't believe the truth will ever be known, and I have a great contempt for history."—George Meade, American philosopher

"Myth, memory, history—these are three alternative ways to capture and account for an elusive past, each with its own persuasive claim."—Warren I. Susman, historian

"History in general is a collection of crimes, follies, and misfortunes among which we have now and then met with a few virtues, and some happy times."—Voltaire

"[Some historians hold that history] is just one damned thing after another."—Arnold Toynbee, twentieth-century historian

"History is a pack of lies about events that never happened told by people who weren't there."—George Santayana, philosopher

"History: An account mostly false, of events mostly unimportant, which are brought about by rulers mostly knaves, and soldiers mostly fools."—Ambrose Bierce, writer

"For what is history, but . . . huge libel on human nature, to which we industriously add page after page, volume after volume, as if we were holding up a monument to the honor, rather than the infamy of our species."—Washington Irving

"The past is a foreign country; they do things differently there."
—L. P. Hartley, writer

"History: gossip well told."—Elbert Hubbard, writer

"God cannot alter the past, though historians can."—Samuel Butler, nineteenth-century writer

"Most history is guessing, and the rest is prejudice."—Will and Ariel Durant, writers

OUR FEARLESS LEADERS

"I desire to go to hell and not to heaven. In the former place I shall enjoy the company of popes, kings, and princes, while in the latter are only beggars, monks, and apostles."—Niccolo Machiavelli's last words

"Any fool can make history, but it takes a genius to write it."—Oscar Wilde

Sometimes they were chosen by the people. Other times, by God (or so they say). Or they might have fought their way to the top. However it happened, a handful of people in the history of the world have ended up leading the rest of us. And these kings, queens, dictators, presidents, and more haven't always acted in the best interests of the people. (Now *there's* a resounding understatement!) Sometimes they're corrupt, demented, or delusional. Or, they're crazy beyond belief.

In fact, history provides many, many (too many) examples of leaders acting in ways that would not adhere to any societal norms. Now, it's one thing if our Aunt Ida has a screw loose; that just means we have to keep her away from the expensive china during holidays. It's a whole other thing if Aunt Ida is a prime minister, president, dictator, senator, queen, etc. Suddenly, her propensity for making her seventeen cats wear miniature hiking boots takes on a new significance. One would think that there were and are systems in place for keeping people like Aunt Ida from running large countries (or even small ones). But if you thought that, you'd be wrong.

So here you have it: the funny, frightening, bizarre, and dysfunctional lives of the people who run the world for us. (God help us all.)

What's in a Name?

How nice to lead your country well and be bestowed with a nickname for eternity. For all intents and purposes, Catherine was indeed pretty great, and William sure did a lot to earn his moniker of "Conqueror." But what if you weren't so great and conquering?

→ Charles the Simple ruled France from 898–922. He was the son of Louis the Stammerer. He succeeded his cousin, Charles the Fat.

→ Ethelred the Unready (983–1016) gained his name for his inability to protect England from the Vikings, even though he had several years to prepare.

→ Louis XV ruled France from 1715–1774. At first he was known as the Well Beloved after nearly dying in 1744. However, his ineffective rule, which was a contributing factor to the French Revolution, and penchant for young women (he had affairs with several women, including five sisters) led to his new nickname by the time of his death: Louis the Well Hated.

→ Grover Cleveland, the only president to serve two nonconsecutive terms, was stubborn, strong-willed, and large—which earned him his nickname, Uncle Jumbo. He was also known as the Beast of Buffalo because of rumors that he beat his wife and mother-in-law (which he didn't).

→ Henry IV was known as one of France's greatest kings . . . and lovers. With more than fifty mistresses and several children, he was known as the Gay Old Spark.

→ Bloody Mary, Queen of England from 1553 until her death in 1558, received her nickname honestly. She had a propensity for burning religious dissenters at the stake.

→ Slick Willie (or Teflon Bill), also known as Bill Clinton, president of the United States from 1992–2000, got his nickname for his ability to dodge the many scandals that rocked his administration.

Old Hickory, Indeed

Andrew "Old Hickory" Jackson got his nickname for being tough as old hickory. Well, just how tough was he? By the time he became president of the United States in 1829, he had been in at least seven duels and had the bullets rattling around in his chest to prove it. As a teenager, he and his brother were captured by the British during the Revolutionary War. During his captivity, he received sword wounds on his hand and head for refusing to shine a soldier's boots. As president, he even survived an assassination attempt. On January 30, 1835, Richard Lawrence, an unemployed and deranged house painter, approached Jackson as he left the Capitol and fired at him. His gun misfired. He then pulled out a second pistol, which also misfired. By this point, Jackson was charging Lawrence. The sixty-seven-year-old president beat the would-be assassin with his cane and had to be restrained by aides.

As badass as all that was, his duel with Charles Dickinson in 1806 was even badder. He let Dickinson shoot first because he knew Dickinson was a better shot anyway. Jackson got hit in the chest, and then took careful aim and killed Dickinson.

SIDE NOTE: At Jackson's funeral in 1845, his parrot had to be removed from the church because it wouldn't stop cursing.

Landslide

Charles D. B. King was president of the West African nation of Liberia from 1920–1930. He was challenged in 1927 during one of his reelection bids by Thomas J. R. Faulkner. King beat him by six hundred thousand votes, which is curious since there were only fifteen thousand registered voters at the time. King made the *Guinness World Records* for most fraudulent election in history.

Jefferson vs. Adams

One might think dirty campaigning a fairly modern invention; however, one of the dirtiest campaigns ever in American politics was the second contested presidential election ever. Thomas Jefferson was opposing John Adams in 1800, and although these two had been friends, by the end of the campaign they were bitter enemies. Adams's Federalists charged that Jefferson cheated his creditors, robbed a widow of her pension, and acted a coward during the American Revolution. Rumors abounded that Jefferson would burn all the Bibles and tear down all the churches in America if he became president. He would also make marriage illegal and force all women to become prostitutes. One newspaper even wrote that if Jefferson became president, "murder, robbery, rape, adultery, and incest will all be openly taught and practiced. The air will be filled with the cries of the distressed, the soil will be soaked with blood, and the nation black with crimes." This was not exactly a ringing endorsement.

He are some other whoppers: He made sexual advances on a friend's wife, had several affairs with married women while in France, and fathered several children with one of his slaves. (His enemies didn't know that last one was true . . .) Perhaps worst of all, his opponents planted a story that he was dead. The report ended up in the *Baltimore American* on June 30: "It was last evening reported that the Man in whom is centered the feelings and happiness of the American people, Thomas Jefferson, is no more." It took at least a week for Jefferson to get the word out that he was, in fact, quite alive.

Meanwhile, Adams's camp was fighting off rumors that he was going to marry one of his sons off to one of King George III's daughters and then turn the United States into a dynasty, with Adams as King John I. Adams was also called "old, querulous, bald, blind, crippled, toothless"—some of which were true! According to "sources," Adams sent his running mate, General Thomas Pinckney, to Europe to procure four European women for their pleasure. Adams was able to dispel this rumor with a clever retort: "I do declare, if this be true, Pinckney has kept them all for himself, and cheated me out of my two!"

The Emperor of Whoopee Cushions

Varius Avitus Bassianus, also known as Heliogabalus, was Roman Emperor from 218–222 CE. He was only around fifteen when he became emperor, which can perhaps explain some of his indiscretions.

➜ He supposedly entered Rome as emperor upon a chariot drawn by fifty naked slaves.

➜ He replaced the god Jupiter with a god of his own choosing and then married a local vestal virgin, which was a flagrant breach of Roman law.

➜ He liked to get party guests so drunk that they'd pass out. He'd then move them to a room filled with toothless leopards, lions, and bears so his friends would have a surprise waiting for them when they awoke.

➜ He is credited with inventing an early type of whoopee cushion. He would place inflated animal bladders under his guests' chair cushions at parties.

➜ He married and divorced five women during his short reign, yet he also had time for his chariot driver Hierocles, whom he called his husband.

Needless to say, Heliogabalus was assassinated at the age of eighteen and was erased from all public records. He is remembered today for his "unspeakably disgusting life."

Dude Looks Like a Lady

Edward Hyde, Viscount Cornbury, third Earl of Clarendon, (1661–1723), had a lot of names as well as a lot of peculiar habits. According to him, all he was trying to do was perform his job as provincial governor of New York and New Jersey. However, he was recalled to England in 1708. Why? His political enemies sent letters back to England that described Cornbury's shortcomings. Was he an inept leader? Yes. Corrupt? A tad. However, the letters reported something else entirely. One stated that Cornbury had an "unfortunate custom of dressing himself in Womens Cloaths and of exposing himself in that Garb upon the Ramparts to the view of the public." He would also sometimes lurk "behind trees to pounce, shrieking with laughter, on his victims." Cornbury also supposedly opened the 1702 New York Assembly clad in a hooped gown with an elaborate headdress and fan—much in the style of Queen Anne. His reply when people remarked upon his attire? "You are all very stupid people not to see the propriety of it all. In this place and occasion, I represent a woman the Queen, and in all respects I ought to represent her as faithfully as I can." A few twenty-first century historians now question whether Cornbury really dressed this way; however, there is a portrait of him in a dress hanging at the New York Historical Society.

Domestic Affairs

While extramarital affairs seem to be part and parcel of being a leader, John F. Kennedy's dalliances deserve a special place in history—especially since biographers are still playing the "did he or didn't he and how often" game. Here's the latest tally: Marilyn Monroe? Yes, but not as much as we think. Judy Campbell, reputed girlfriend of Mafia boss Sam Giancana? Big, scary yes. Jayne Mansfield? Yes. Angie Dickinson? Most likely, though she's been coy about it. Mimi Beardsley, nineteen-year-old White House intern (hmm . . . sounds familiar)? Yup. How about his wife's appointment secretary? Of course. Two press aides (at the same time)? Why not?! Ellen Rometsch, prostitute and probable East German spy? Yes—*gulp*.

Not one to let an international crisis get in the way of a good time (see previous sentence), Kennedy had time for some flirting during the Cuban Missile Crisis. While Kennedy was in the Oval Office with his Chiefs of Staff and Cabinet members nervously awaiting a response from Soviet Premier Nikita Khrushchev, a woman walked in with some files. Kennedy stopped what he was doing to check her out. As she left the office, Kennedy turned to Secretary of Defense Robert McNamara and asked who she was. McNamara answered, "She's filling in today." Kennedy promptly asked him for her name and phone number.

Some researchers contend that Kennedy's sexual appetite may have been caused in part by the drug he was taking for Addison's disease, which listed among its side effects "increased virility."

Kennedy even described what it was like for him to England's Prime Minister Harold Macmillan: "If I don't have a woman for three days, I get terrible headaches."

Poor George

Even though George Washington was a fine general and a highly regarded president, he still had his detractors. It was rumored that he had an illegitimate son, that Alexander Hamilton was his illegitimate son, that he had a British spy mistress, and that he had a romantic relationship with a young women whom he liked to call "pretty little Kate, the washer-woman's daughter." A man named George Washington Bowen even claimed to be the son of the father of our country and a prostitute. He wasn't.

A Slave to Love

Richard Johnson was a hero in the War of 1812, a congressman (1804–1819), and a senator (1819–1829) representing Kentucky. He was also Martin Van Buren's vice president (1837–1841), and unlike other politicians of the day, he had no problem letting folks know that he was in a romantic relationship with one of his slaves. In fact, he considered Julia Chinn, a light-skinned slave he inherited from his father, his common-law wife. Now, before you begin thinking of Johnson as a brave man who followed the laws of love above the laws of the land (it was illegal for a white person to marry a black person back then), read on. When Chinn died in 1833 of cholera, Johnson took up with another of his slaves. When she left him and ran off with another man, Johnson hired someone to capture her, and then he promptly sold her at auction. Oh, we're not done. Then he began a relationship with the newly sold slave's sister.

SIDE NOTE: Johnson had what is perhaps the worst campaign slogan of all time. While running for vice president, he campaigned with this nugget: "Rumpsey Dumpsey, Rumpsey Dumpsey, Colonel Johnson killed Tecumseh." (He supposedly killed the Shawnee chief during the War of 1812.)

Genghis Certainly Khan

The Mongol Emperor Genghis Khan (1162–1227) once said, "The greatest joy a man can know is to conquer his enemies and drive them before him. To ride their horses and take away their possessions. To see the faces of those who were dear to them bedewed with tears, and to clasp their wives and daughters in his arms." Well, according to a study in an article called "The Genetic Legacy of the Mongols," Khan took his "clasping" seriously. The article states that nearly 16 million men living today in Asia carry Khan's Y-chromosome, which means about 0.5 percent of the male population of the world is descended from Genghis Khan or his brothers.

Nero's Greatest Hits

Nero Claudius Caesar Augustus Germanicus was Roman Emperor from 54–68 CE and was known for his many tyrannical acts. However, he is probably best remembered for something he didn't do: sing and play his lyre while Rome burned. In fact, he was out of town at the time, but returned upon hearing the news and personally took part in search and rescue operations. He also opened his palaces for the homeless and made sure survivors had provisions. Not bad for a guy who killed his mother and stepbrother, threw the requisite orgies, and started the whole Roman leader fad of persecuting Christians. He blamed them for the fire (deflecting the blame that was being placed on him) and, in the words of the ancient historian Tacitus, "covered with the skins of beasts, they were torn by dogs and perished, or were nailed to crosses, or were doomed to the flames and burnt, to serve as a nightly illumination when daylight had expired."

Oh, but that's not all! What did Nero do with the area that had been destroyed by the fire? He built a gigantic palatial estate for himself. Named *Domus Aurea*, or Golden House, this one to three hundred–acre complex featured a pool the size of a lake, buildings shaped like cities, ceilings that rained perfume and flowers on guests, and a 120-foot statue of the man himself. Upon its completion, Nero supposedly said, "Good, now I can at last begin to live like a human being."

Perhaps worst of all, Nero fancied himself an actor and singer. He gave public performances in which no one was allowed to leave until he was finished. Another ancient historian, Suetonius, wrote that pregnant women who went into labor had to give birth during his recitals and that men pretended to die so they could be carried out.

Foundering Fathers

America's Founding Fathers were the leaders who in words and deeds fought to create the United States of America. They signed the Declaration of Independence, fought in the Revolutionary War, and framed the Constitution. Today, they are revered as manly heroes with bad teeth who walked around wearing stockings and wigs. But, like the rest of the leaders in this chapter, they, too, acted badly.

ALEXANDER HAMILTON

THE GOOD: First US secretary of the treasury, aide-de-camp to George Washington during the Revolutionary War, and author of the *Federalist Papers*.

THE BAD: Became embroiled in a love affair with Maria Reynolds. Reynolds's husband blackmailed Hamilton during the affair, even trying to secure a job in government from Hamilton. Hamilton published a detailed confession of his affair (too much information, Alex!) that shocked his constituents and his wife and damaged his reputation.

THE UGLY: Fought a duel with Aaron Burr and died.

GEORGE WASHINGTON

THE GOOD: First president of the United States.

THE BAD: As a young man, wrote several love letters to a married woman. Did anything physical happen between the two? Nobody knows for sure.

THE UGLY: He never chopped down a cherry tree and he didn't have wooden teeth. (His falsies were carved from hippopotamus and elephant ivory.)

THOMAS JEFFERSON

THE GOOD: Author of the Declaration of Independence, third president of the United States, and overall Renaissance man.

THE BAD: First president to propose the idea of a formal Native American removal plan. He also, according to historian Richard Morris, "detested intellectual women." While giving a free pass to Abigail Adams, Jefferson was annoyed by "the political chatter of women in Parisian salons," and wrote, "The appointment of a woman to office is an innovation for which the public is not prepared, nor am I."

THE UGLY: While officially against slavery and the slave trade, he not only kept slaves and most likely fathered children with one of them, but he also believed blacks were inferior to whites "in the endowments both of body and mind."

BENJAMIN FRANKLIN

THE GOOD: Scientist, author, inventor, and US ambassador to France.

THE BAD: Womanizer and father to an illegitimate son who remained loyal to the British during the Revolutionary War.

THE WEIRD: Threw parties where guests had to drink from glasses wired to batteries. They'd get a shock after each sip. He'd also electrocute turkeys to the amazement of his guests and then feed it to them.

JOHN ADAMS

THE GOOD: First vice president, second president, delegate to the Continental Congress, and good ol' Puritan at heart.

THE BAD: Signed the Aliens and Sedition Acts, which allowed the president to deport any foreigner he thought dangerous to the country and made it a crime to publish "false, scandalous, and malicious writing" against the government.

THE UGLY: Called "the crankiest Founding Father" by historian Jack D. Warren, Adams was a hater who had a gripe with just about everyone. Called Benjamin Franklin "the old conjurer" and fought with him throughout their lives. He believed Washington didn't deserve the adoration he received and that Washington's greatest talents were his looks, graceful movements, and his gift of silence.

The Dog Shogun

Tokugawa Tsunayoshi (1646–1709) was the fifth shogun of the Tokugawa dynasty of Japan. He was known as a religious man and a very strict ruler. And he liked dogs. Born in the Year of the Dog, he felt canines should be treated well. In a series of edicts on "Compassion for Living Things," Tsunayoshi commanded his people to protect dogs at all costs. Under these edicts, if you injured, killed, or even ignored a dog, you could be put to death or be forced to commit suicide.

At one point, three hundred people were put to death in one month for failing to live up to the edicts, and anywhere from sixty thousand to two hundred thousand people were killed or exiled during Tsunayoshi's reign for violations. Soon the city became so overrun with dogs that Tsunayoshi had fifty thousand dogs sent out from the city to live in special kennels where they were fed rice and fish each day—all at taxpayers'

I Like Big Butts

Ibrahim I was Sultan of the Ottoman Empire from 1640–1648. In the short time he ruled, he nearly single-handedly destroyed it all. He supposedly suffered from stress, though his obsession with extremely obese women may have relieved some of it. He sent his attendants out to find the largest woman possible. They returned with a 330-pound woman from either Armenia or Georgia. Ibrahim named her "Sheker Pare" (piece of sugar), gave her a government pension, and made her Governor General of Damascus. He supposedly drowned all 280 women in his harem after a rumor that another man had slept with some of them. Ibrahim was also seen feeding coins to the fish that lived in the palace's pool. He was strangled to death in a coup in 1648.

William the Corpulent Conqueror

When one thinks of kings and queens, brave deeds, loyal attendants, and dignified ceremonies usually come to mind. None of these were in the cards for William the Conqueror, who suffered a fate worthy of a Monty Python skit. After attacking a French garrison in 1087, the once strong (and now fat) William got thrown off his horse and ruptured his intestines on the metal pommel at the front of his saddle. It took a little while to die, but once he did, things only got worse for the king. First, his attendants ran off after stripping the body of all valuables and removing all the king's weapons and furniture. Then, during William's funeral procession, his pallbearers had to drop him to go fight a fire. Finally, the king's giant body, which had swollen considerably, didn't fit in the stone sarcophagus reserved for him. The bishops attending the body pushed and squeezed to no avail. Finally, the stomach burst, showering everyone with dead body pieces. Everyone in the church made a run for it.

NOTE: Late in life, William fought more bravely in the dining room than on the battlefield. He became so corpulent that King Philip I of France said that he looked like a pregnant woman.

Bad Dad

Peter I of Russia (1672–1725) deserved being called "the Great" for many reasons. He was the father of Russian modernization and expansion that transformed Russia into an empire and major European power. Unfortunately for Alexei, Peter was also father of . . . Alexei. Brought up by his mother, who didn't much care for Peter, Alexei was torn from her at age nine, when Peter sent her to a convent. Alexei fled Russia as an adult, and when suspected of masterminding a plot to overthrow the tsar, he was tracked down, captured, and returned to his home country for a few rounds of torture. Alexei confessed during the torture, and died before he could be put to death. Thanks, Dad!

Nice Day for a Dwarf Wedding

In October 1710, the same Peter the Great had the pleasure of marrying off his niece Anna Ivanovna to Friedrich Wilhelm, Duke of Couland. He threw a lavish banquet that lasted two days. Soon after, he held another lavish wedding, this time for the royal dwarf Iakim Volkov and his dwarf bride. See, the six-foot, seven-inch tsar had a thing for dwarfs. Some might say he collected them. He had dwarf servants and entertainers surrounding him. He liked surprising his guests by having naked dwarfs jump out of giant pies, and some historians say he was interested in breeding a race of small people. So, needless to say, this dwarf wedding was a big deal for the tsar.

Back in August of 1710, he had instructed all the dwarfs in Moscow to be rounded up and sent to St. Petersburg. They were "given" to the lords and ladies of his court, who were told to care for them and make sure they were dressed in the latest Western fashion. When the wedding took place in November, seventy dwarfs were in attendance. During the ceremony, the full-sized guests remained on the sidelines and laughed—especially since Peter made sure that elements of the wedding resembled his niece's recent nuptials. At the feast, the dwarfs sat at miniature tables in the center of the hall, while again the full-sized guests watched from the sidelines, roaring with laughter as the dwarfs danced, drank, and even brawled. Crazy? Certainly. Mean-spirited? Definitely. But was there a deeper meaning to his madness? Could it be that Peter was using the dwarf wedding as a mirror held up to the laughing lords and ladies, who, though they thought themselves cultured, couldn't yet hold a candle to the European elite? Hmm . . .

SIDE NOTE: Not to appear overly attentive to people of diminutive stature, Peter also threw a wedding for a seven-foot, six-inch giant named Nicolas Bourgeois who he found in France. He then located a Finnish giantess for Nicolas, but since giants were more difficult to find than dwarfs, Peter didn't insist on a basketball player wedding party. The tsar was disappointed when the couple didn't produce any huge children, but he kept Bourgeois on salary just to have him show up at his wacky parties and ceremonies . . . sometimes dressed as a baby.

Making Uncle Peter Proud

Anna Ivanovna, Peter the Great's niece, ruled Russia from 1730 until her death in 1740. She didn't care much for actually ruling Russia, but she enjoyed parties and tormenting the aristocracy. Her court included a nobleman who was not only forced to be her fool, but also had to pretend to be a chicken—all the time. But that wasn't enough. She ordered an ice palace built for a marriage that she arranged (she liked arranging and throwing lavish weddings) between this "fool" and one of her elderly maids. Anna wasn't done yet! The bride and groom had to dress as clowns, and then they and the wedding party had to sleep naked in the ice palace during a typically freezing-cold Russian night.

Executive Obsessions

NOSOCOMEPHOBIA: Richard Nixon was deathly afraid of hospitals. In 1974, he initially refused to go to a hospital to get treatment for a blood clot. He said at the time, "If I go into the hospital, I'll never come out alive." (Wonder what the word for "fear of Richard Nixon" is.)

TAPHEPHOBIA: George Washington had no problem risking his life for American independence from Britain, but he was terrified by the prospect of being buried alive. Upon his deathbed in 1799, he made one of his attendants promise that his body would be left alone for two days after expiring, just in case. (But then again, due to the primitive nature of medical care at the time, it did happen every once in a while and wasn't such a bizarre thing to be scared of.)

AEROPHOBIA: Kim Jong Il won't fly anywhere due to his fear of flying. He travels mostly on his personal rail car. He has traveled as far as Moscow this way. Kim "got" his fear honestly: He was in a helicopter crash in 1976 in which he was seriously injured. Ronald Reagan and Joseph Stalin were also afraid of flying.

CLAUSTROPHOBIA: Muammar al-Qaddafi supposedly freaks out in confined spaces and is much more comfortable remaining outdoors in a tent than checked into a hotel. While attending a United Nations General Assembly meeting in 2009, Qaddafi tried to set up his tent in New York City in several different locations (Donald Trump even offered him some land to use).

AILUROPHOBIA: Afraid of cats? Then you're an ailurophobe . . . just like Napoleon Bonaparte. Other famous ailurophobes included Alexander the Great, Genghis Khan, Adolf Hitler, Julius Caesar, and Benito Mussolini.

CYNOPHOBIA: Chancellor Merkel of Germany was bitten by a dog as a child, and has been deeply afraid of dogs since. Former Russian Prime Minister Vladimir Putin, with this information in hand, once offered a dog as a gift to the chancellor. He would also let his black Lab sit in on their meetings.

TRISKAIDEKAPHOBIA: He may have said, "The only thing you have to fear is fear itself," but Franklin Delano Roosevelt was afraid of something else: the number thirteen. He avoided hosting dinner parties with thirteen people, and he refused to travel on the thirteenth.

The Glass King

Charles VI was crowned King of France in 1380 at just eleven years old. At first, he was called Charles the Beloved, but by the end of his life, he was Charles the Mad. Most likely he suffered from schizophrenia, especially since his psychotic episodes began in young adulthood and included paranoid delusions.

His first known episode happened in 1392 while on a personal mission to avenge the attempted murder of one of his advisors. As he and his escort traveled through a forest, a page dropped the king's lance, which made a loud noise. Charles drew his sword and yelled, "Forward against the traitors! They wish to deliver me to the enemy!" He then began hacking away at his small army, killing at least one knight and, most likely, several more. When finally wrestled to the ground, he quickly went into a coma.

Charles recovered, but his bouts continued. Other episodes included forgetting that he was king, not remembering his wife, claiming his name was George, running through the corridors of his palace (to the point where the entrances were barricaded), refusing to bathe or change his clothes for five months, thinking he was made of glass, and more. Charles died in 1422, and he most likely passed his illness to his grandson, Henry VI of England.

SIDE NOTE: Henry VI, King of England and disputed King of France, at one point became completely unaware of *anything* that was going on around him. This lasted for more than a year.

Take Me to Your Leader

Not one but two future presidents of the United States had close encounters with unidentified flying objects. We'll begin with Jimmy Carter's sighting. In 1969, while governor of Georgia, Carter claims that he and several other men were standing outside the Lion's Club in Leary, Georgia, when they saw a strange red and green orb in the sky. I'll let Jimmy tell you the rest.

> "I don't laugh at people anymore when they say they've seen UFOs. It was the darndest thing I've ever seen. It was big, it was very bright, it changed colors, and it was about the size of the moon. We watched it for ten minutes, but none of us could figure out what it was. One thing's for sure: I'll never make fun of people who say they've seen unidentified objects in the sky. If I become president, I'll make every piece of information this country has about UFO sightings available to the public and the scientists."

This was part of his speech at the 1976 Southern Governors Conference while campaigning for president.

Meanwhile, Ronald Reagan was the first US president to talk about the world uniting against a threat from "a power from outer space." Some may have thought he was just losing his marbles, but he was speaking from personal experience. His first encounter happened before he was governor of California. He was on his way to a party at actor William Holden's home in Hollywood when he and his wife, Nancy, pulled over to watch a strange light in the sky. They arrived at the party and told everyone of their UFO sighting. Reagan's second sighting was in 1974 while aboard the governor's private plane. They were heading toward Bakersfield, California, when one of his aides noticed a bright white light near the plane. Everyone aboard, including the pilot, watched in amazement as whatever it was then shot upward very quickly. Reagan actually told the story to the Washington Bureau Chief of the *Wall Street Journal*, Norman

C. Miller. "It was a bright white light. We followed it to Bakersfield, and all of a sudden, to our utter amazement, it went straight up into the heavens." Miller verified the amazing claim with the pilot, who corroborated it.

Family Matters

If aliens invade (or just come for a short visit), we'll want to impress them with our fearless leaders. But for every Lincoln, Churchill, and Clinton, there are at least a couple Billy Carters in the woodwork. These are the people related to the important people, the ones who show who we really are as a race: numbskulls and imbeciles, drunkards and liars, failures and egomaniacs. In other words, they are a lot more human than their overachieving relatives.

➔ He was a gifted student, a high-school basketball star, devout Christian, successful farmer, and—oh yeah—president of the United States. How can one live up to an older brother like that? In Billy Carter's case, you don't. During Jimmy Carter's presidency, his younger brother, Billy, was often in the news, and always for the wrong reasons. Known as a colorful, hard-drinking, good ol' boy with his "Redneck Power" T-shirt, Billy first cashed in by endorsing Billy Beer, the first (and only) beer named for a president's family member. He was then caught urinating on an airport runway in full view of the press and foreign dignitaries. He once participated in and judged a world championship belly flop competition. Finally, there was Billygate (one of the first of many "-gates" to follow Watergate): Billy accepted money from the Libyan government in return for his influence with his brother. He was eventually registered as a foreign agent of the Libyan government.

➔ Mary Todd Lincoln, Abraham Lincoln's wife, was known to be slightly unhinged, and later in life she was actually institutionalized by her son Robert. For one thing, she had a clothing obsession: in one four-month period she supposedly bought three hundred pairs of gloves. She was quick to anger and often took it out on her husband: at least once she threw stove wood at him, and another time chased him out of their home in Springfield, Illinois, with a butcher knife. She also spent exorbitant amounts of money redecorating the White House while the Civil War was going on.

➔ Thomas Jefferson's brother Randolph seemed like a nice enough fellow. Thomas clearly loved him and helped him out financially throughout his life. However, while Randolph, like his famous brother, graduated from the College of William and Mary, he evidently did not share his brother's genius. A former Monticello slave, Isaac Jefferson, recalled in 1847 that Randolph was "one mighty simple man (who) used to come out among black people, play the fiddle, and dance half the night." Some historians believe it is Randolph and not Thomas who sired children with the slave Sally Hemings.

➔ Sam Houston Johnson was the younger brother of President Lyndon Johnson and, like Billy Carter, lived in his brother's immense shadow. Sam had a drinking problem, and when he was drinking, he liked talking—to anyone who would listen, particularly the press.

Lyndon solved the problem temporarily by forcing his brother to live at the White House so he could keep an eye on him. When returning to the White House (which Sam called "the penitentiary") after a night of drinking, Sam would look for some cameras, hold his wrists together as if they were cuffed, and yell, "Back to my cell!"

➜ Richard Nixon's brother Don dreamed of starting a fast-food chain called Nixonburgers. He accordingly accepted and never repaid a $200,000 loan from Howard Hughes. Richard, his paranoid brother, consequently had his brother's phone tapped.

➜ Neil Bush has the distinction of being an embarrassment to two presidents. As a son of one president and brother to another, Neil brought to the table shady business dealings, liaisons with prostitutes, a savings and loan scandal, several poorly run businesses, and a messy divorce that included allegations of voodoo. The historian Kevin Phillips said in a *Washington Post* story on Neil, "He's incorrigible. He seems to be crawling through the underbelly of crony capitalism."

Ah . . . Caligula

I bet you were wondering when I'd get to this guy. Of all the crazy rulers throughout history, Caligula's the one who set the bar so high for all the other mentally unstable monarchs, dictators, and presidents out there. Caligula ruled the Roman Empire from 37–41 CE, which isn't a long time to get your crazy on, but he worked quickly as he took Rome on a wild ride, until his own bodyguards finally had the good sense to assassinate him.

He rose to the throne amidst the usual political maneuvering and bloodletting and was widely hailed at first as "our star." The ancient historian Philo describes the first seven months of Caligula's reign as "completely blissful." He granted bonuses to the troops, recalled political exiles, threw gladiator battles for the populace, and even focused his attention on political reform. Then something happened. Some historians say he had a brain fever. Others argue that Caligula, much like his distant cousin Alexander the Great, suffered from epilepsy, and that after an unusually violent attack, Caligula was a changed man. Here's an incomplete list of some of the crazy and cruel actions attributed to Caligula:

→ Accused his father-in-law, Gaius Silanus, and Gemellus, grandson of the previous emperor, of treason and forced them to commit suicide.

→ Kept his favorite horse, Incitatus, inside the palace in a stable carved out of ivory. He threw parties in the horse's name and the horse dined with the guests. His attempts to install his horse as a priest and consultant are usually seen today as attempts at humor and mockery.

→ Had hundreds of ships tied together to make a nearly three-mile temporary floating bridge so he could ride across the Bay of Naples on horseback, which he did for two straight days. Why?

Supposedly as a child, a seer said he had no more chance of becoming emperor than of crossing the bay of Baiae on horseback. He showed them!

→ Announced he was a god and ordered the building of temples and statues in his honor. He sought to force the Jews to worship him and even ordered statues of himself to be placed in the Temple of Jerusalem. (These plans were wisely never carried out.) He was known to dress up as Apollo, Mercury, and even Venus.

→ Opened a brothel in the imperial palace.

→ Used spectators as lion bait when the games he was throwing ran out of criminals. Five rows of fans were pulled into the arena and devoured.

→ Declared war on Poseidon, god of the ocean, and brought back chests full of worthless seashells as booty.

→ Beat a citizen who insulted him with a heavy chain—every day for three months. He only stopped because the man had become so gangrenous that he smelled horribly. So Caligula had him beheaded.

→ Tortured countless people. He was partial to sawing people by filleting them at the spine. Or he'd restrain a prisoner upside down and chew on his testicles while the prisoner was still in ownership of them.

➜ Most likely committed incest with all three of his sisters. When one of his sisters died, he had her deified.

SIDE NOTE: Caligula, whose real name was Gaius Julius Caesar Augustus Germanicus, was nicknamed "Caligula" as a baby by Roman soldiers. His father, the general Germanicus, would take the young boy with him on military campaigns and dress him up in a miniature soldier's uniform. The soldiers called him "little soldier's boot," or Caligula.

An Emperor's Appetite

Justin II, Byzantine Emperor from 565–578 CE, had a lot on his plate. War (most of it disastrous for his empire), political restlessness, and financial ruin finally took a toll on Justin, and he cracked. Before abdicating the throne, he had taken to biting his attendants while being pulled through his palace on a wheeled throne. In fact, rumor has it he didn't just like biting people—he also liked eating them.

The Fairy-Tale King

Most likely not mad—merely eccentric—Ludwig II, King of Bavaria, ruled from 1864 until his death in 1886. He hated public functions, insisting on watching full-scale operatic performances by himself because he didn't like people staring at him. He liked traveling the countryside to converse with the common folk he met along the way. He also used all of his personal fortune to build several elaborate, fairy-tale castles. Ludwig built the Residenz Palace in Munich, complete with an elaborate winter garden with a lake on the roof; New Swan Stone Castle, a Romanesque fortress in his hometown of Hohenschwangau, featuring wall paintings depicting scenes from Wagner's operas; Linderhof Castle, an ornate neo-French rococo-style palace; and Herrenchiemsee, a replica of Louis XIV's seven hundred–room palace at Versailles that was never finished because Ludwig ran out of money. He also had plans for several other over-the-top palaces.

Ludwig racked up millions in personal debt, and that, along with his eccentricities, was enough for conspirators to seek to get rid of him. A laundry list of bizarre behavior was compiled (including childish table manners, making his groomsmen dance naked at moonlit picnics, and talking to imaginary friends), doctors were engaged to pronounce Ludwig insane, and on June 10, 1886, a government commission deposed the king. By the thirteenth, he was dead. To this day, no one knows if he committed suicide or was murdered. He is remembered favorably today, especially by Germany's tourist industry.

SIDE NOTE: Ludwig's brother Otto became king next; however, he never truly ruled because he suffered from severe mental illness. I can't verify this story, but it's too good to pass up. The insane king-in-name-only supposedly started each day by shooting a peasant. His attendants, not wanting to upset him but not wanting to make a daily sacrifice either, made sure the pistol was loaded with blanks, and then they'd dress someone up like a peasant and have them drop dramatically to the ground after the shot.

Quick Comebacks

➜ While campaigning for the presidency, someone once threw a cabbage at William Howard Taft. He quickly responded, "I see that one of my adversaries has lost his head."

➜ Dorothy Parker, seated next to President Calvin Coolidge at a dinner, supposedly remarked, "Mr. Coolidge, I've made a bet against a fellow who said it was impossible to get more than two words out of you." He replied, "You lose." Upon his death, Parker was said to have remarked, "How can they tell?"

➜ During the Civil War, President Lincoln was annoyed at general George McClellan's hesitancy to engage the enemy. Lincoln wrote to him, "If you don't want to use the army, I should like to borrow it for a while."

➜ "When the president does it, that means that it's not illegal." —Richard Nixon

➜ "I have left orders to be awakened at any time in case of national emergency, even if I'm in a Cabinet meeting."—Ronald Reagan

➜ "I have often wanted to drown my troubles, but I can't get my wife to go swimming."—Jimmy Carter

The Blunder of the World

Frederick II of Hehenstaufen was one of the most powerful Holy Roman Emperors of the Middle Ages. He was known as the Wonder of the World for his incredible knowledge and curiosity, love of literature and science, his skeptical views about religion, and for his ability to speak at least six languages. While ruling much of Europe and throwing together the occasional Crusade, he had time for indulging his curiosity with some fairly cruel (even by Middle Ages standards) science experiments.

➜ As a linguist, he wished to know whether people were born with a natural language that was suppressed when they learned the language of the land. In other words, what language did Adam and Eve speak? Hebrew? Greek? Latin? Frederick sought to answer this question by ordering a number of infants raised without any adults talking to them—at all. He ordered, "foster-mothers and nurses to suckle and bathe and wash the children, but in no ways to prattle or speak with them." The experiment was considered a failure, for "the children could not live without clappings of the hands, and gestures, and gladness of countenance, and blandishments."

➜ As a religious skeptic, Frederick wanted to know if humans had a soul. So he shut a prisoner up in a cask to see if the soul could be observed escaping a hole in the cask as the prisoner died.

➜ How does digestion work? Well there's one way to find out: "He fed two men most excellently at dinner, one of whom he sent forthwith to sleep, and the other to hunt; and that same evening he caused them to be disemboweled in his presence, wishing to know which had digested the better: and it was judged by the physicians in favour of him who had slept."

(All quoted material is from the thirteenth-century Italian Franciscan Salimbene's *Chronicles*.)

Hobbies and Quirks

These hobbies and quirks of our leaders wouldn't necessarily make them unfit for office, although they should raise a few eyebrows.

→ King Charles II, ruler of England in the 1600s, collected mummies of dead Egyptian pharaohs. He liked to cover himself in mummy dust, hoping it would make him as great as they were.

→ John Quincy Adams liked to relieve the stress of the presidency with an early morning swim. Each morning he would remove his clothing and jump in the nearby Potomac River. (Yes, times were different back then.) One morning, a reporter named Anne Royall snuck up on the president, snatched his clothes, and sat on them. She said she would only give the clothes back if he gave her an interview. Adams loathed talking to the press, but he answered her questions while standing deep in the river. This was perhaps the first presidential interview conducted by a female reporter. Teddy Roosevelt also swam naked in the Potomac—with members of his Cabinet.

→ James Garfield was the first ambidextrous president of the United States. However, not only could he write with both hands, if you asked him a question, he could simultaneously write the answer in ancient Greek with one hand and Latin with the other.

→ Warren Harding had a bit of a gambling problem. At one point he lost a whole set of White House china while playing poker. His advisers were known as the Poker Cabinet. Harding was also particularly fond of Laddie Boy, his pet Airedale. Laddie had his own servant and sat at his own chair during Cabinet meetings.

→ Calvin Coolidge liked to hide in the White House shrubbery and then jump out and scare his Secret Service agents. Coolidge also had an electronic horse installed in the White House. He rode it every day. Finally, Coolidge also enjoyed wearing Indian headdresses and Boy Scout uniforms, and he had a pet raccoon that liked to reside on his shoulders.

→ Jimmy Carter may have been considered the first US "bubba" president, but not only did he study nuclear physics in college, but he can read two thousand words a minute.

→ Kim Jong Il, the de facto leader of North Korea (the official leader being his long-dead father), loves movies. His collection of videotapes and DVDs is said to be twenty thousand and growing. His favorite movies include the James Bond series, anything featuring Godzilla, Rambo, Clint Eastwood's *In the Line of Fire*, and the Friday the 13th movies. In 1978, he had South Korea's most famous movie

director, Shin Sang-ok, kidnapped (along with his movie star wife). He then forced them to make movies for North Korea until they escaped in 1986.

Violence in the House

These days, the most dangerous thing that can happen to a wayward US senator, congressman, or other politician is that they end up in jail. That wasn't always the case.

On May 22, 1856, Preston Brooks, Democratic congressman from South Carolina, walked into the Senate chamber to find Senator Charles Sumner of Massachusetts at his desk. Brooks said, "Mr. Sumner, I have read your speech against South Carolina, and have read it carefully, deliberately, and dispassionately, in which you have libeled my state and slandered my white-haired old relative, Senator Butler, who is absent, and I have come to punish you for it." Brooks then proceeded to beat Senator Sumner senseless with a metal-tipped cane.

Sumner, who was angry about the escalation of violence in Kansas over the issue of whether to admit Kansas to the Union as either a free or proslavery state, called the proslavery militia from Missouri "murderous robbers." He then went on to slam Butler, saying that he spat and stammered when he talked, which was in a sense true, since Butler had had a stroke. Butler's cousin, Brooks, then took matters into his own hands.

The inch-thick cane was smashed to splinters, and the bloody Sumner cried out, "I am almost dead, almost dead." Brooks was finally restrained. The resulting Senate hearing failed to muster enough votes to expel Brooks; however, he resigned. Then he ran for reelection to fill the vacant seat he had just vacated. He won. Meanwhile, it took Sumner three years to recover from the attack. Brooks received many new walking sticks from his supporters.

More Violence in the House

On January 30, 1798, two congressmen who didn't care for each other, Matthew Lyon (a Republican from Vermont) and Roger Griswold (a Federalist from Connecticut), started shouting at each other. (Nothing new there.) Then things took a turn for the worse when Lyon spat tobacco in Griswold's face after Griswold called him a coward. The Federalists moved to expel Lyon, and the House spent two long weeks debating it. Lyon apologized and the House fell short of the number of votes needed for expulsion.

The next day, Griswold, who was obviously not happy with the apology or the vote, decided to settle the matter himself. He rushed across the House floor and, with his brand-new hickory walking stick, began beating on Lyon. Here is Griswold's account: "I gave him the first blow—I call'd him a scoundrel and struck him with my cane, and pursued him with more than twenty blows on his head and back until he got possession of a pair of tongues [i.e. tongs], when I threw him down and after giving him several blows with my fist, I was taken off by his friends."

Here's an even better account from Representative George Thatcher of Massachusetts: "I was suddenly, and unexpectedly interrupted by the sound of a violent blow. I raised my head, and directly before me stood Mr. Griswald [sic] laying on blows with all his might upon Mr. Lyon, who seemed to be in the act of rising out of his seat. Lyon made an attempt to catch his cane, but failed—he pressed towards Griswald and endeavored to close with him, but Griswald fell back and continued his blows on the head, shoulder, and arms of Lyon [who] protecting his head and face as well as he could then turned

and made for the fire place and took up the [fire] tongs. Griswald dropped his stick and seized the tongs with one hand, and the collar of Lyon by the other, in which position they struggled for an instant when Griswald tripped Lyon and threw him on the floor and gave him one or two blows in the face."

One House member said Congress had been reduced to "an assembly of gladiators." Griswold, not content to leave things alone, got in the last word: "I might perhaps have given him a second beating but the House was called to order."

Even More Violence in the House

➜ Even thought it was outlawed, by the late 1700s dueling had become an accepted (if idiotic) form of resolving political disagreements and preserving honor. Even Abraham Lincoln was once challenged to a duel. Lincoln chose swords as the weapon, and thankfully all was resolved before the duel. Nevertheless, there were dozens of duels from the 1700s until around the end of the Civil War, when dueling finally fell out of favor. Politicians killed in duels included the governor of Georgia in 1789, Alexander Hamilton (1804), Senator Armistead Mason of Virginia (1819), US District Attorney Joshua Barton (1823), North Carolina Congressman Robert Vance (1827), and more!

➜ The threat of violence during congressional sessions was so real that by 1835, Vice President Martin Van Buren wore a brace of pistols when presiding over the Senate.

→ John Fox Potter, Republican congressman from Wisconsin just prior to the Civil War, had a nickname. He was called "Bowie Knife" Potter due to an incident during the spring of 1860. Basically he offered to fight Roger Pryor, congressman from Virginia on the following terms: "Bowie-knives and a dark room, and one of us to die." The duel never took place, but Potter received several Bowie knives as gifts from sympathizers (including a four-pound, six-and-a-half–foot folding knife) as well as a nifty new nickname.

→ In one of the last physically violent episodes in US politics, Strom Thurmond of South Carolina and Ralph Yarborough of Texas wrestled for more than ten minutes outside a Senate hearing room over the 1964 Civil Rights Bill. Both were sixty-one years old at the time, but Thurmond, who was quite physically fit, pinned Yarborough at least twice.

Tricky Dick Tricked by Dick

Dick Tuck has been a political consultant for American politicians for more than fifty years. And although he has worked on political campaigns for Adlai Stevenson, John and Robert Kennedy, and many others, he is best known as a political prankster and Richard Nixon's arch nemesis. Many historians called Nixon's administration paranoid, and if that were indeed the case, Dick Tuck had a hand in making it that way. Here's a list of some of Tuck's Nixon pranks.

→ In 1950, while Nixon was running for California senator, Tuck, who was working for Nixon's opponent, got himself hired as a Nixon campaign worker. Tuck was put in charge of organizing campaign rallies. At one such rally at UC Santa Barbara, Tuck booked an extremely large auditorium (a capacity of four thousand), yet did very little to promote the event. Fewer than fifty people attended. When the speech was over, Nixon asked Tuck his name and told him, "Dick Tuck, you've made your last advance."

→ In 1956, during the Republican National Convention where Nixon was running for reelection as Eisenhower's vice president, Tuck hired garbage trucks to drive by the convention center with signs that read "Dump Nixon."

→ After the first Kennedy-Nixon debate in 1960, Tuck hired an elderly woman to don Nixon buttons and approach Nixon as he got off the plane. While TV cameras were rolling, the woman hugged him and said, "Don't worry, son! He beat you last night, but you'll get him next time."

→ During the 1960 presidential campaign, Nixon went on a whistle-stop tour of California. While giving a speech on the caboose, Tuck allegedly disguised himself as a railway employee and waved the train out of the station while Nixon was still talking.

→ In a 1962 campaign visit to Chinatown, San Francisco, Nixon spoke to a crowd while children holding welcome signs stood behind him. However, Tuck planted one sign that said "What about the Hughes loan?" which was a reference to a loan the reclusive billionaire Howard Hughes made to Nixon's brother. Nixon grabbed the sign and ripped it up . . . on camera. (This prank backfired slightly when Tuck found out later that the sign actually said, "What about the *huge* loan?)

➔ In 1968, Tuck hired a pregnant African-American woman (some accounts say he hired several pregnant women) to wear a T-shirt with Nixon's slogan and walk through a Nixon rally. What was the slogan? "Nixon's the One."

➔ Tuck is mentioned in the Nixon tapes! An October 1972 Oval Office tape caught Nixon saying, "Dick Tuck did that to me. Let's get out what Dick Tuck did!"

➔ Many historians say that Nixon's desire to out-Tuck Tuck led to his department of dirty tricks and the resulting Watergate scandal. During the Senate Watergate Committee hearings, Nixon's former chief of staff, H. R. Haldeman, passed Tuck at the Capitol and said, "You started all of this." Tuck replied, "Yeah, Bob, but you guys ran it into the ground."

Note: Tuck ran for a California senate seat in 1966. His campaign slogan was, "The Job Needs Tuck and Tuck Needs the Job." When he lost, his concession speech included this gem: "The people have spoken . . . the bastards."

Lord of All Beasts

Although he was known as the Butcher of Uganda for his brutal rule of the country during the 1970s, he preferred to be known as His Excellency President for Life, Field Marshal Al Hadji Doctor Idi Amin, VC, DSO, MC, Lord of All the Beasts of the Earth and Fishes of the Sea, and Conqueror of the British Empire in Africa in General and Uganda in Particular. During his reign, he had around three hundred thousand people tortured and/or killed. And although it has been debated, it's been reported that he kept the heads and other body parts of some of his victims in a refrigerator and once told his minister of health that he found human flesh rather too salty.

SIDE NOTES:

➜ Amin was Uganda's light heavyweight boxing champion from 1951–1960.

➜ After receiving a message from God in a dream, Amin decided to make Uganda a "black man's country." He expelled the up to eighty thousand Indians and Pakistanis in the country.

➜ He wore specially designed tunics that were lengthened so that he could wear more World War II medals.

➜ Amin wiped out entire villages and had their bodies thrown in the Nile. Workers had to keep fishing the bodies out in order to stop the ducts at a nearby dam from becoming clogged.

➔ In 1974, he praised Adolf Hitler and condemned the Jews in front of the United Nations General Assembly.

➔ In 1976, he declared himself "the uncrowned King of Scotland." He also liked to wear kilts.

➔ Amin once wrote to Britain's Queen Elizabeth, "Dear Liz, if you want to know a real man, come to Kampala."

➔ After the British broke diplomatic relations with his regime, Amin said he had beaten the British, and then considered himself Conqueror of the British Empire.

➔ The United States didn't end diplomatic relations with Amin until 1978—seven years into Amin's reign of terror.

A Real Stinker

"Maybe if I hadn't been so fastidious, I could have changed history," Lina Basquette once remarked. But she would have had to put up with a lot. . . .

Basquette was an American actress known for her long-ranging career, which began in the silent film era, and her nine marriages. She received a fan letter from Adolf Hitler in 1929 that proclaimed her his favorite movie star after seeing her performance in *The Godless Girl*. In 1937, she was even invited to Germany, and she accepted. She met with Hitler and reported that he made a pass at her. Basquette recounted, "The man repelled me so much. He had terrible body odor; he was flatulent. But he had a sweet smile, and above all, he had these strange penetrating eyes." When Hitler got too close for her comfort, Basquette declared that she kicked him in the groin and then told him she was part Jewish. There was no one else present, so it's impossible to corroborate the story; however, in a 1989 profile, the *New Yorker* found all the other claims she made about the visit to be accurate. Plus, it's an awesome story, and if it isn't true, it should be.

Behind Every Strong Man . . .

➜ Rutherford B. Hayes's wife, Lucy, began the beloved tradition of the Easter Egg Roll at the White House. She, however, was not so beloved of State Department officials because of her insistence on not serving alcohol at state dinners. The officials nicknamed her Lemonade Lucy and spiked oranges with rum punch behind her back and served them with dinner.

➜ President William McKinley's wife, Ida, hated the color yellow and banned it from the White House. She even ordered gardeners to pull up all the yellow flowers. Ida suffered from seizures, though that didn't stop her from crocheting hundreds of slippers for veterans of the Civil War: blue slippers for Union vets and gray for Confederate vets. Nobody got any yellow slippers, that's for sure.

➜ Who was one of the most powerful woman of the sixteenth century? Diane de Poitiers, mistress to King Henri II of France. Henri was married to Queen Catherine, but he let Diane sign documents, appoint ministers, and even hand out titles. A British medical journal reported in 2009 that de Poitiers most likely died from consuming too much gold, which at the time was believed to preserve one's youth.

➜ Edith Wilson, wife of President Woodrow Wilson, was so traditional in her views that she was against women's suffrage. But that didn't stop her from continuing with her husband's administration after he suffered a debilitating stroke. She lied to Congress and said Wilson was only suffering from "temporary exhaustion," and then set it up so that all memos and correspondences from the president's cabinet went through her. This went on for several months. Edith was also a ninth-generation descendant of Pocahontas.

➜ After the assassination attempt on President Ronald Reagan, his wife, Nancy, would consult with an astrologer to tell them which days were good and which should be avoided. This advice would then affect the president's schedule to the point that his chief of staff, Donald Regan, complained. She worked tirelessly for Regan's dismissal. Nancy also controlled access to the president and encouraged him to hold conferences with Soviet General Secretary Gorbachev.

➜ John Wayne Gacy, democratic party activist, director of Chicago's annual Polish Constitution Day Parade, volunteer clown, and notorious serial killer, met with first lady Rosalynn Carter twice in 1978. They had their picture taken together both times, and she signed one of them, "To John Gacy, Best Wishes." The signed photo later became a major embarrassment to the United States Secret Service because Gacy was wearing an S pin in the photo, which indicated that he had received special clearance from the Secret Service.

Presidential Pets

"If you want a friend in Washington, get a dog."—attributed to Harry Truman

Over the years, the US presidents have brought much with them to the White House: their wives, their children, their grandchildren, their mothers-in-law, their obsessions, and best of all . . . their pets.

➜ Thomas Jefferson had more than thirty White House pets, including two grizzly bear cubs. They were a gift from the explorer Zebulon Pike. The bears didn't stick around for long, as Jefferson saw fit to send them to a museum in Philadelphia.

➜ John Quincy Adams kept a pet alligator in the East Room of the White House. It slithered around and chased visitors. He also had silkworms.

➜ Andrew Jackson kept fighting cocks. No word if he had any cock fights at the White House.

➜ Martin Van Buren kept two tiger cubs for a short time.

→ The Lincolns let their sons Willie and Tad keep their pet goats in their rooms. They also had dogs, a rabbit, a horse, and a turkey.

→ Andrew Johnson fed the white mice he found in his White House bedroom.

→ Benjamin Harrison had a goat, a collie, and two opossums named Mr. Reciprocity and Mr. Protection.

→ Teddy Roosevelt's brood brought a veritable zoo to the White House. Their animal retinue included badgers, mice, raccoons, pigs, parrots, dogs, cats, baby bears, snakes, a one-legged rooster, a kangaroo rat, and a Shetland pony named Algonquin that once had the pleasure of riding the White House elevator. Oh yeah, I almost forgot the spotted hyena named Bill. It was a gift from the emperor of Ethiopia, and Roosevelt taught it tricks and let it beg for scraps at the dinner table.

→ William Taft had two cows, Mooly Wooly and Pauline Wayne. At least one of them lived in the White House kitchen, since Taft was quite fond of fresh milk. Really fresh.

→ Woodrow Wilson kept a herd of sheep that he let graze on the White House lawn. He also had a ram named Old Ike that liked to chew tobacco.

→ Calvin Coolidge had Rebecca and Horace, raccoons; Ebenezer the donkey; Smoky the bobcat; Tax Reduction and Budget Bureau,

lion cubs; Billy the pygmy hippo; several dogs; canaries; a wallaby; a small antelope; and a black bear.

➜ Herbert Hoover one-upped J. Q. Adams by bringing *two* crocodiles to the White House.

➜ Franklin Roosevelt once accidentally left his Scottish Terrier, Fala, behind when visiting the Aleutian Islands. Roosevelt was criticized after then spending thousands of dollars to send ships back to find the dog. As Roosevelt was running for his fourth term in office, he had to address the issue. He said, "You can criticize me, my wife, and my family, but you can't criticize my little dog. He's Scotch, and all these allegations about spending all this money have just made his little soul furious." All was then forgiven, and he won the presidency.

→ Lyndon Johnson got into trouble when he was photographed holding up his two beagles, Him and Her, by their ears.

WHEN THINGS WERE ROTTEN

"History is little else than a long succession of useless cruelties."—Voltaire

A quick look back at our past would make one think that our ancestors had it a tad rougher than we did. Okay, let's face it: Things back then sucked! Disease. Torture. Victorian England. It's a wonder we've made it this far. So travel back with us now (five miles through the snow, uphill both ways) to a few of the trifling difficulties our forebears endured.

Wife for Sale . . . Barely Used

Single woman in England during the Middle Ages? No problem! You could own property and sign your name to contracts. Married? Sorry, but you are now property of your husband. As one legal entity, as defined by a legal doctrine called *coverture*, you would be completely subordinated to your husband.

William Blackstone described it best in the late eighteenth century: "By marriage, the husband and wife are one person in law: that is, the very being or legal existence of the woman is suspended during the marriage, or at least is incorporated and consolidated into that of the husband: under whose wing, protection, and cover, she performs every thing."

So . . . if you were the property of your husband, could he sell you? Of course! Toward the end of the 1600s all the way through the early twentieth century, there were numerous stories of men selling their wives at auction. Here's one titillating glimpse gathered by *Ancestors* magazine: "Rodney Hall, a labouring man of idle and dissolute habits . . . led his wife into the town with a halter round her body . . . he led her twice round the market, where he was met by a man named Barlow, of the same class of life, who purchased her for eighteen pence and a quart of ale."

The magazine goes on to report that in 1897, a shoemaker "on a drinking spree at Irthlingborough" ran out of money and sold his wife so he and his friends could keep drinking. Nice.

Dying Aid

It was low in calories (not that the Romans were counting), it had a sweet taste, and it killed you. Yes, it seems that in ancient Rome, the perfect diet aid was also the perfect *dying* aid. A popular way to sweeten wine was to throw in some sugar of lead (lead acetate), which was made by boiling grape juice in lead pots. The resulting syrup, called *defrutum*, was then concentrated again into *sapa*—yummy, but deadly. Friends, Romans, and countrymen used sugar of lead in their wine or to preserve fruit. It probably didn't help that wine was often served in lead cups.

Speaking of Deadly

Mercury is the only metal that's liquid at "standard conditions," which is why civilization has always been fascinated with its silvery awesomeness. So even though it's extremely toxic, it has been used as a medicine for centuries. It has been found in Egyptian tombs dating back 3,500 years. In China, it was thought to prolong life, heal broken bones, and prevent pregnancy. (It prevented pregnancies the way it prevented long life.) Other cultures used it as a cosmetic and medicine. "Blue mass," which was a pill with mercury as a main ingredient, was prescribed in the 1800s for constipation, depression, and toothaches. In the twentieth century, kids were given mercury as a laxative. As far as we know, the only thing mercury cures you of is life.

Favorite Forms of Torture

→ The mechanical flagellator, invented in the early eighteenth century in England, could service forty people at the same time. Talk about service!

→ Gossip much? During the 1500s, the British had a neat little device called the scold's bridle or branks. It was a cage that locked around a woman's head. The cage also had a spiked plate that was inserted in the mouth to curb the tongue, literally. If that wasn't enough, the gabber was then sometimes led through the streets on a leash.

→ During the Middle Ages, if you were told to sit on the Judas Cradle, you were in big trouble. Basically, it was a stool with a wooden pyramid on the top. Guess where you had to sit.

→ Need a confession? Nothing was as effective during the Middle Ages as the rack. Place the guilty party (you know he's guilty!) on the wooden frame, tie his arms to the ropes on the top and his legs to the ropes on the bottom. Turn the handle and wait for your captive to "stretch" the truth.

→ The brazen bull was used by the ancient Greeks. Basically, you threw your guilty party in a hollowed-out bronze statue of a bull, closed the trapdoor, lit a fire underneath the statue, and, well, that was about it. When that got boring, the Greeks invented a system of tubes so the victim's screams sounded like an angry bull.

→ The Spanish tickler didn't tickle. This simple device consisted of a pole and a metal claw, which was used to "dig" for the truth.

→ The chair of torture consisted of a chair covered with spikes. Need we say more?

→ Devices that need no explanation: the knee splitter, the head crusher, the breast ripper, rat torture, and thumbscrews.

➔ Finally, good luck if you were a crook in the fourth century. A person accused of a crime would be forced to close his hand around a red-hot poker. However, this wasn't the punishment. If his or her hands healed after three days, they were declared innocent.

SIDE NOTE: In seventeenth-century France, the remains of executed murderers were considered good-luck charms. After a good hanging or burning at the stake, crowds would swarm over the remains looking for some luck.

Bedlam

The word "bedlam" means a place of confusion and uproar, and it's derived from the name of England's most infamous hospital: Bethlem Royal Hospital. It's been around since the 1300s, and even though today it's known for its humane psychiatric treatment, it's renowned for its centuries of cruelty.

From the time it began accepting inmates . . . I mean, patients . . . with mental illnesses in the 1350s until the early twentieth century, the hospital was a veritable madhouse. Patients were often chained to the walls or floor, with one patient having been chained for fourteen years. "Treatment" also including whipping, dunking, and more. Refusing to take your medicine? No problem! The staff at Bethlem had specially designed metal keys they used to force your mouth open. For a time in the eighteenth century, the hospital charged a penny to visitors who could walk past the cells containing the chained patients and view the "freaks of Bethlem." It was a popular tourist attraction, and many had fun "making sport and diversion of the miserable inhabitants."

Eat Your Hearts Out, Sports Fans!

➜ The ancient Aztec and Maya Indians of Central America played a game that looked a lot like lacrosse. Except, if your team lost, your captain had his heart removed and passed around for fans to eat. Another game they played was called *ullamaliztli*, which was played with a heavy, solid rubber ball. Like soccer, you couldn't use your hands to control the ball, but neither could you use your feet. Instead teams batted the ball around with their hips and buttocks. What happened with the losing team? See above.

➜ After ransacking a village, the Vikings would often resort to a game of tug-of-war to decide who got the plunder. The catch? The two teams would face off with a roaring fire between them. The winners would get the loot. The losers burned.

➜ *Pankration* was an ancient Greek wrestling match with a twist— there were no rules (or clothes). You could kick, scratch, wrestle, choke, tell your opponent to "Look at that pretty lady in Row B!" and then sucker punch him . . . whatever. It was considered bad form to kill your opponent.

➜ *Soule* was a popular game played by peasants in Normandy, Brittany, and Picardy from the twelfth through the nineteenth centuries. The rules were simple: Two teams of up to a thousand participants each had to get a large ball into the opponent's net or onto their side. The game usually got violent and could last for several days—especially since the goals could be separated by miles of farmland, forests, meadows, rivers, etc.

Whip It Up

Imagine it's the 1600s and you're tutor to the heir to the throne. It's a pretty good gig, but what in heaven's name do you do if the prince acts up or decides not to finish his lessons? Because of the doctrine of the divine rights of kings, which stated that a monarch has ultimate authority over man (which he got directly from God), you couldn't exactly spank the royal's highness. One solution was to assign a whipping boy. This poor kid, usually of high birth, would be raised alongside the prince, and every time the prince acted up, the whipping boy would be physically punished in front of the prince.

Meanwhile, in Ancient Greece, if a natural disaster struck (such as a famine, disease, or invasion), they would choose a *pharmakos* to take the blame. The *pharmakos* would usually be a beggar or a cripple, and he would be cast out of the community, stoned, or beaten to death so that the disaster would go away.

Cure Nones

These days, the only thing truly scary about going to the doctor is the bill. However, the history of medicine and doctors is full of cures that did more to kill you than cure you. The ancient Egyptians, Africans, and Europeans all thought that epilepsy and mental illnesses could be cured by drilling a hole into your skull. This would release the demons from your head, and if you were lucky enough to survive, you got to keep the skull fragment they removed as a lucky charm. Back in the day, you could go to the barber for a haircut and a nice, healthy bloodletting, which was used to cure all sorts of maladies, such as fevers, colds, cancer, and of course, excessive bleeding!

In February 1685, we have what can be described as the worst cure ever. (And proof that peasants had a better chance at recovering from an illness than the aristocracy.) King Charles II of England suffered either a stroke or some sort of kidney dysfunction. All the royal doctors were summoned, and they immediately embarked on a treatment regimen that would have killed several healthy people. First, the bloodletting. Then they induced vomiting. Followed by an enema. When all that didn't work, over the course of the five days it took the king to die, the good doctors filled his nose with snuff, let out some more blood, singed the king's shaved scalp with burning irons, daubed his feet with pigeon poop, drilled a hole in his skull, applied heated cups to the skin (which formed blisters), applied more enemas, let out even more blood, fed him the gallstone from a goat, gave him a dose of forty drops of human skull, and more. And for all that, the king apologized: "I am sorry, gentlemen, for being such a time a-dying."

What a Pig

Louis XI, king of France in the 1400s, liked animals. When he wasn't hunting them, torturing them, or having them captured for his large zoo, he had them sing for him. In 1450, having grown tired of dressing up his pigs in clothing and wigs and sticking them with pins, he ordered the Abbot of Baigne to create a new musical instrument that incorporated pigs into its design. The abbot did as he was told, and before you knew it, there it was: a piano-type instrument that, when you played a key, stabbed a pig with a spike, making it cry. The pigs were arranged by the pitch in which they screamed, and by all accounts, the songs played were recognizable and the king and his attendants enjoyed the show immensely.

SIDE NOTE: When Louis XI was feeling especially cruel, he ordered a game of manhunt in which prisoners were covered with deerskin and then chased and torn apart by the king's hounds.

ANOTHER SIDE NOTE: The inventor Athanasius Kircher designed a similar device in 1650—except he used cats. Here's a description in the inventor's own words (from his *Musurgia Universalis*): "In order to raise the spirits of an Italian prince burdened by the cares of his position, a musician created for him a cat piano. The musician selected cats whose natural voices were at different pitches and arranged them in cages side by side, so that when a key on the piano was depressed, a mechanism drove a sharp spike into the appropriate cat's tail. The result was a melody of meows that became more vigorous as the cats became more desperate. Who could not help but laugh at such music? Thus was the prince raised from his melancholy."

Dangerous Fashion Statements

As I write, today's most popular fashion statement is skinny jeans. And as with any fad, it must soon be followed by the medical condition it causes. Skinny jeans are said to cause *meralgia paresthetica*, which is also known as tingling thigh syndrome. *The New England Journal of Medicine* also warns of *jeans folliculitus*, which is a skin rash. Well, fashion throughout the course of history has been dangerous, as well as deadly. But remember, before you laugh at our ancestors, remember those skinny jeans.

➜ Shoe fashion throughout history seemed more about danger than anything else. In Europe during the 1300s, the aristocracy began wearing shoes with long, pointed tips. (The best were shaped to look like male genitals and stuffed with fabric.) As the nobility were always seeking to outdo one another, the shoes got longer and longer until everyone at court was tripping all over the place. Instead of coming to their senses, however, they took care of the problem by tying the tips of their shoes to their legs with rope.

➜ High heels have been around for quite some time. In sixteenth-century Europe, women's heels reached the incredible height of two to three feet! These shoes, called *chopines*, proved useful since they kept women's dress hems clean when walking along the poop-filled streets. (Where do you think the maids emptied the chamber pots, anyway?) The Catholic Church also approved, since if you can barely walk, surely you can't dance . . . and if you can't dance, well . . . This fashion statement fell out of favor eventually as women needed something to hold on to (a maid or a long cane) at all times, and they kept falling over and severely hurting themselves.

→ Louis XIV reigned France from 1643–1715. At the height of his powers in the early 1700s, the diminutive Louis wore high heels to make himself appear taller. Soon, it was all the rage, and all the aristocracy was wearing them. Louis's heels were often up to five inches high, and as the royal court made theirs bigger, so did he. Soon everyone was tottering around until Louis decreed that no one else's heels could be bigger than his.

→ Foot binding was utilized in China for around a thousand years to emulate fashionable tiny feet. It involved breaking the arch and then wrapping the foot, resulting in an approximately three-inch foot from toe to heal, as well as a lifelong disability. By the nineteenth century, nearly 100 percent of upper-class women had bound feet. It was outlawed by the Communist party in 1949.

→ France loved Benjamin Franklin's lightning rod so much that a Parisian designer in the 1770s began making hats with lightning rods attached to them—complete with grounding wire.

→ The ancient Egyptians and Romans used cosmetics containing mercury and lead.

→ It was fashionable during the seventeenth and eighteenth centuries for women to have pale white skin and red rouged cheeks.

They achieved the pale look with white lead, which caused skin eruptions. They then covered up the eruptions with more lead. Lady Mary Coventry, a famous London society hostess, died at the age of twenty-seven of lead poisoning. In the early twentieth century, women used arsenic to give their skin a luminous glow and the deadly nightshade to brighten their eyes and enlarge their pupils.

→ Eighteenth-century Europe saw the advent of gigantic wigs decorated with all sorts of things: stuffed birds, fruit, sculptures, and more. These wigs often attracted bugs, mice, and other critters. The highlight was most probably Marie Antoinette's giant, four-foot high ship wig.

→ Corsets have been used for hundreds of years. In the 1550s, Catherine de Medici, wife of King Henry II of France, ordered her ladies in waiting to keep their waists extremely thin. They used corsets made of steel, wood, or ivory to keep their queen happy. According to many historians, the whole myth of women as the weaker sex was due to the fact that their corsets were restricting their lung capacity. So when excited, unable to breathe adequately, they fainted. Lungs weren't the only body parts affected by waist-reducing corsets. The stomach, bladder, ribs, and more were all compressed—causing great discomfort and poor health.

→ The Padaung tribe of Burma (Myanmar) and Thailand view long necks as beautiful. Beginning at age five, a brass coil is added to a girl's neck. Over the years, the coil is replaced with longer ones, as it slowly pushes the collarbone down and compresses the rib cage. This gives the illusion of the giraffe neck that's been all the rage there for hundreds of years.

Now THAT'S a Curse

In March 1657, a Japanese priest cremated a cursed kimono that had been owned by three girls—all who died before wearing it. Instead of releasing the evil spirit in the kimono, however, strong winds blew the kimono to the floor and the house caught on fire. And before you could say "Don't play with fire," the "Long-Sleeved Kimono Fire" destroyed 75 percent of the city of Edo (now Tokyo), and more than one hundred thousand residents perished.

The Real Dracula

Yes, Virginia, there was a real Dracula, but he was much, much worse than a vampire. Vlad Drakulya III, Prince of Wallachia (a region in what is now southern Romania) ruled on and off from 1448–1476. If listing his attributes, "nice" wouldn't crack the top thousand. Cruel, sick, and murderous? Getting warmer.

We have to remember that times were different then, and rulers needed to be tenacious in order to hold on to what was theirs. After ruling for a mere two months in 1448, Vlad was overthrown. He returned in 1456, killing the man who had taken his place. At this point, Vlad realized he needed to make some changes. Crime was rampant, his castle nearly in ruins, and political intrigue was everywhere. One of his first steps was to enslave the boyars (local aristocracy) who had opposed him and force them to rebuild his castle. The ones who didn't die from exhaustion were killed. For his fight against crime, he devised some simple deterrents. If you were caught stealing, you had the skin of your feet removed and then your feet were sprinkled with salt. Goats licked the salt off. One story reports that Vlad was so confident that his punishments worked that he placed a golden cup in the central square of Tirgoviste . . . where it remained untouched for years.

Vlad also enjoyed burning or boiling people, hammering nails into heads, and cutting off limbs; however, his preferred method of torture was impalement. Vlad the Impaler would attach each of his victim's legs to a horse, place the tip of a sharpened stake where the sun don't shine, and say, "Giddyap!" He would impale thousands of people at a time and arrange the stakes in geometric patterns around one of his cities. One of the most famous woodcuts of Vlad shows him feasting with dozens of impaled victims in the background.

Vlad also thought it important that everyone contribute to the welfare of the kingdom. So one day he invited all the vagrants, beggars, and cripples of the land to a great feast. After the meal and a short speech from Vlad, he had the hall boarded up and set on fire. That's one way to eradicate poverty . . .

SIDE NOTE: In Romania, he is considered one of its greatest leaders, and in 2006, Vlad the Impaler was voted one of the "100 Greatest Romanians."

Inferiority Complex?

In the late 1600s, Peter the Great of Russia wanted his traditional, long-bearded countrymen to look more like smooth-faced Europeans. When banning beards proved difficult (some believed you couldn't get into heaven without an untrimmed beard), he instead imposed a beard tax. Nobles were required to pay one hundred rubles per year. Commoners paid less. He also taxed long Russian coats, trying to encourage the shorter French style, and changed the Russian calendar to follow the Julian one. (Imagine thinking the year was 7207, only to have your king change it to 1700.)

Bad Fad

On February 12, 1933, a twenty-one-year-old Japanese student (some sources place her age at nineteen) killed herself by jumping into the crater of Mount Mihara, an active volcano on the island of Izu Oshima. This started a trend in Japan, and suddenly tourists were flooding the island not to see the crater, but to witness the suicides. Hundreds killed themselves before authorities thought to put up a fence around the crater.

Rotten Religion

"How many evils have flowed from religion!"—Lucretius

➜ The ancient Aztecs believed that the sun would disappear without food. What did the sun eat? Human hearts. Lots of them. Meanwhile, priests sacrificed crying children so their tears would appease the rain god. And not to be outdone, their maize goddess required a virgin be killed and skinned. A priest would then dance wearing her skin.

→ In the thirteenth century, a young shepherd claimed to have been visited by Jesus, who told him to go on a Crusade to liberate the Holy Land. Thousands of French children followed him to the docks, where French merchants agreed to take them all to Jerusalem. The merchants then sold all the children into slavery.

→ In 1096, thousands of Christians marched to free the Holy Land from infidels. They weren't led by a child, however; they were, instead, following a goose. There's no word on whether or not the goose of God approved of the army killing all the Jews they met on the way. Thousands were brutally murdered.

→ Back in the Middle Ages, the Catholic Church decided it was immoral for women to sing or act on stage. So who would sing the girl parts? No problem! The Church castrated young boys so their voices wouldn't change as they grew older.

→ What did William Tyndale do to deserve both strangulation *and* being burned at the stake? He was arrested by church authorities in 1535 for translating the Bible into English, which was against the law. Only Latin translations were legal, meaning only educated people could read it. A lot of Tyndale's translation was eventually used to create the 1611 King James version of the Bible, which is still in use today.

"HISTORY" AND OTHER LIES

"Clio, the muse of history, is as thoroughly infected with lies as a street whore with syphilis."—Arthur Schopenhauer, *Parerga und Paralipomena*

"To look back upon history is inevitably to distort it."
—Norman Pearson

We rely on our historical record for a sense of what happened in the past, who we were and are today, where we came from and why. So perhaps the most unsettling aspect of history is just how little of it is true. There's so much myth mixed up with our history, we might as well call it mythtory. And whether or not this mythmaking is accidental or purposeful, once it's out there, it's almost impossible to reign it in. In today's digital age, we have the historians correcting the record, and then we have other historians correcting the corrected record, and so on. This chapter highlights some of our most cherished beliefs about historical figures and events, and then shows you why you are wrong to ever repeat these tidbits as truth again. (Until someone else comes along and tells us we were wrong.)

Magellan Circumnavigated the Truth

Not only did Magellan fail to circumnavigate the globe, it wasn't even the point of his voyage. In 1519, Ferdinand Magellan, a Portuguese captain in the service of Spain, set out with five ships to find a safe way to the Spice Islands. However, the three-year tour turned into a horror show of storms, mutiny, starvation, and war. Magellan was killed in the Philippines by natives, ships had to be burned and left behind, crew were captured, etc., until finally in 1522, one remaining ship limped into a Spanish harbor with fewer than twenty of the original crew members aboard. They were never paid their full wages.

Betsy Fraud

There's no easy way to say this . . . Betsy Ross did not design the first American flag. George Washington did not, in June 1776, visit Betsy's upholstery shop at 239 Arch Street with a rough sketch and ask her to complete and execute the design. The story didn't even exist until 1870, when William J. Canby told this captivating tale to the Pennsylvania Historical Society. Who was William J. Canby? Betsy Ross's grandson. While it's true that Ross sewed uniforms and flags for the Continental Army, it's unlikely there was an approved United States flag earlier than 1777. Historians claim this story gained popularity because Philadelphia was preparing for its centennial celebration and it jived with the patriotic mood in the city.

Would Not, Could Not with a Horse

Catherine the Great, Empress of Russia, was not crushed to death while having sex with a horse. (Yes, she had her lovers, but they were all human.) In fact, she passed away (very boringly, I might add) in bed. Basically, Catherine was the object of an eighteenth-century smear campaign launched by the French soon after her death. Those quick to debunk the horse myth sometimes state Catherine died on the toilet. That, too, is untrue. She may have passed out in the bathroom, but she didn't die there.

Let Them Eat Their Words

Sorry, but Marie Antoinette never said, "Let them eat cake."

The story goes like this: In 1789, France was undergoing an economic depression and bread was scarce. A crowd of poor French mothers marched to Versailles to plead with Louis XVI. While the angry mob gave Louis a piece of their minds, Marie supposedly said, "If they have no bread, let them eat cake."

First of all, taken in context, what Marie meant was that at that time, when bakers ran out of cheap bread, by law, they had to sell their better bread at the same price as the cheaper bread. One type of expensive bread was *brioche*, which is often translated as "cake." Second, she didn't say it, anyway. In fact, the writer Jean Jacques Rousseau wrote in his book *Confessions*, "I remembered the thoughtless saying of a great princess, who on being informed that the country people had no bread, replied, 'Then let them eat cake.'" The great princess couldn't have been Marie Antoinette, since *Confessions* was published twenty-three years before Marie's fictitious suggestion. Most likely this rumor was started by antiroyalists.

Why Is Paul Revered?

Sure, Paul Revere played a part in the American Revolution. But why is he the one (and only one) remembered for the midnight ride when it was actually up to forty different messengers raising the alarm about the Redcoats coming? On the night of April 18, 1775, he and another man, William Dawes, were told to ride from Boston to Lexington to warn John Hancock and Samuel Adams that British troops were heading out to arrest them and then capture weapons stored in Concord. Both Revere and Dawes made it to Lexington, warning patriots along the way, although Revere did not yell, "The British are coming!" (That would have alerted British patrols, duh!) On the way to Concord, Revere was captured by the British. Dawes and Samuel Prescott (who joined them on the ride) both escaped, but only Prescott made it to Concord in time to alert the militia.

Revere didn't become the hero of the midnight ride until nearly forty years after his death. In fact, his obituary didn't even mention it. But when Henry Wadsworth Longfellow wrote the poem "Paul

Revere's Ride" in 1861, everything changed. You know the poem, even if you don't think you know it:

> Listen, my children, and you shall hear
> Of the midnight ride of Paul Revere,
> On the eighteenth of April, in Seventy-Five;
> Hardly a man is now alive
> Who remembers that famous day and year.

Longfellow's poem was treated as history for nearly one hundred years. It appeared in textbooks and historians referred to it. Unfortunately, Longfellow made a lot of it up. Using his poetic license, he got the lantern signals mixed up; sent Revere all the way to Concord, even though he never made it that far; and perhaps worst of all, he neglected to mention any of the other heroes from that night. So basically, he used Revere's name because it rhymed better than *Dawes* or *Prescott*.

In 1896, Helen F. Moore, angry that William Dawes had been forgotten by history, wrote a parody of the poem:

> 'Tis all very well for the children to hear
> Of the midnight ride of Paul Revere;
> But why should my name be quite forgot,
> Who rode as boldly and well, God wot?
> Why should I ask? The reason is clear—
> My name was Dawes and his Revere.

Napoleon's Feet

We all think we know about Napoleon Bonaparte—Emperor of France, great military commander, and famous person of short stature. In fact, these days, many people ignore the first two facts and focus on his height. (I mean, there aren't many basketball players suffering from a Napoleon complex, eh?) History placed Napoleon at five feet, two inches tall, and indeed that is true . . . if you're using the old French foot, which was longer than the English foot. After doing the conversion math, Napoleon was actually five feet, six inches or so. No giant, but perfectly average for the eighteenth and nineteenth centuries.

Allegiance to What???

Millions of schoolchildren in the United States start the day off with a half-hearted rendition of "The Pledge of Allegiance." It's an oath of loyalty to flag, country, and principles (such as states' rights, small government, low taxes, etc.), but it was penned by a devout socialist. Francis Bellamy was a Baptist minister (who once delivered a sermon called "Jesus Was a Socialist"), Christian socialist, and cousin of socialist utopian novelist Edward Bellamy. The poem appeared in a popular children's magazine in 1892 as a way to sell flags to public schools and boost the magazine's circulation. Now *there's* an American ideal we can all pledge to!

The original hand instructions for the pledge called for the right hand to be removed from the heart at the mention of the word "flag" and extended outward toward the flag. This ended during World War II because it looked too much like a Nazi salute.

Bad Call

Abner Doubleday wasn't the biggest name to come out of the Civil War, but he was involved in many key battles as a Union officer. He is, however, one of the biggest names in baseball—known far and wide as the inventor of the game. Too bad he had nothing whatsoever to do with its invention.

A committee was formed in the early twentieth century to determine the origins of baseball. Instead of attempting to find the truth, the committee wanted a feel-good story that proved baseball was a red-blooded American sport. The report stated, "The first scheme for playing baseball, according to the best evidence obtainable to date, was devised by Abner Doubleday at Cooperstown, New York, in 1839." Their evidence was a single letter from a man named Abner Graves, a mentally unstable man who later killed his wife. A prolific writer, Doubleday left no notes or mention of even playing baseball. Also, he was at West Point in 1839, as his family had moved from Cooperstown the previous year.

In 1953, Congress set out to correct this inaccuracy by officially crediting the invention of modern-day baseball to Alexander Joy Cartwright, a volunteer firefighter and member of the New York Knickerbocker Base Ball Club. He supposedly was the first to draw a diagram of a baseball diamond and write down the rules on which baseball is based. Legend has it he also taught the game to people he met while traveling to California during the Gold Rush. Though he did play for the Knickerbockers, there is written proof that the rules for the game already existed and that Cartwright's descendants simply exaggerated his role.

So who invented baseball? Nobody. It evolved over time from a children's stick and ball game played in England for centuries.

Lizzie Borden

> Lizzie Borden took an axe
> And gave her mother forty whacks.
> And when she saw what she had done,
> She gave her father forty-one.

Now it's no big stretch to say that a popular schoolyard chant is historically inaccurate, but since it's all most people know about Lizzie Borden, it's probably a good exercise to clear up the facts here. First off, Lizzie's stepmother was the one murdered, and she only received eighteen or so whacks from an axe. Her father received only eleven. Also, though Lizzie was indeed accused of these murders, she was acquitted—mostly because police refused to use a new-fangled crime prevention tool: fingerprinting.

The Rub on the Tub

On December 28, 1917, journalist H. L. Mencken published a fictitious history of the bathtub in the *New York Evening Mail*. In it, he
wrote that the bathtub was introduced into the United States in the
1800s and that Americans didn't take to bathtubs until President
Millard Fillmore had one installed in the White House. He wrote
it to "have some harmless fun in war days"; however, he soon began to find his "preposterous 'facts' " in other newspapers, medical
literature, and reference books. Mencken wrote years later: "The
success of this idle hoax . . . vastly astonished me. It had, of course
no truth in it whatsoever, and I more than once confessed publicly
that it was only a jocosity . . . Scarcely a month goes by that I do not
find the substance of it reprinted, not as foolishness but as fact, and
not only in newspapers but in official documents and other works
of the highest pretensions."

Some historians think Mencken was up to more than some
harmless fun. They believe that he was out to prove that Americans would believe any nonsense as long as it appealed to their
imagination or emotions. Whatever his motives, this "fact" is still in
circulation to this day.

The Tribe That Was . . . or Wasn't . . . or Was

Manuel Elizalde, Jr., a Philippine government minister, announced
to the world in 1971 that he had discovered a Stone Age tribe that
had had no contact with the outside world. The tribe, called the

Tasadays, lived in caves, wore leaves for clothing, used stone tools, and didn't have a word for "enemy." The tribe was featured on the cover of *National Geographic* and received worldwide attention. After scientists started asking questions, Philippine President Ferdinand Marcos declared the tribe off-limits. In 1986, after Marcos was deposed, a Swiss anthropologist and two journalists searched for the Tasadays and found members of a local tribe who said they pretended to be a Stone Age tribe at Elizalde's instructions. However, in a different interview, two Tasaday members who had originally claimed they were bribed by Elizalde admitted they had also been bribed by journalists with "cigarettes, candy, anything we wanted—if we would say what he told us to." So what's the truth? No one truly knows.

The War of Breakfast Foods

In 1683, as one hundred thousand Ottoman Turks besieged the city of Vienna, the bakers of the city, who had to be up early in the morning to make the bread, heard what sounded like digging. Indeed, the Turks were attempting to tunnel under the city's walls. The bakers raised the alarm and the Turks were unable to take Vienna before King John III of Poland showed up and drove them away. Legend has it that the bakers celebrated the end of the siege by creating a commemorative pastry in the shape of the Turks' flag—a crescent moon. It was called a *kipfel*, which is German for *crescent* . . . now commonly known as the croissant. Meanwhile, the bakers, unable to contain their excitement, also created a new roll in the shape of a stirrup to honor King John. The Austrian word for stirrup is *bugel*—which is where we could have gotten the word *bagel*. Unfortunately, neither story is true.

Corrections to the Historical Record

→ There is no William Tell, and he didn't shoot an apple off his son's head.

→ Richard III, King of England from 1483–1485, was not a hunchback. Paintings of him were touched up after his death to make it look like he was. He also didn't murder his brother, his son, or his wife. He can thank Tudor slander and a hack named Shakespeare for turning him into such a villain.

→ Here are two shockers: Vikings didn't wear helmets with horns attached to them, and pirates didn't make people walk the plank.

→ Most people in the 1490s knew the world was round. Columbus didn't have to convince anyone. Also, the first European to discover America was Bjarni Herjolfsson in the late 900s.

→ Lady Godiva didn't ride through the streets of Coventry naked.

→ "Ring Around the Rosie" does not refer to the Great Plague.

→ The great pyramids were not built by slaves. Excavated skeletons show that the builders were actually Egyptian laborers who were paid for their work.

→ Benjamin Franklin told the story of flying a kite with a key attached to the string, but never did it.

→ Charles H. Duell, Commissioner of the US Patent Office, did not say, "Everything that can be invented has been invented."

WAR STORIES

"[History is a] mixture of error and violence."—Johann Wolfgang von Goethe

"The direct use of force is such a poor solution to any problem, it is generally employed only by small children and large nations."—David Friedman

"If it's natural to kill, why do men have to go into training to learn how?"—Joan Baez, singer/songwriter

"I think war might be God's way of teaching Americans geography."—Ambrose Pierce

I've read in a couple of different places that during the last 3,500 years, the world has had around 230 years when there were no wars. I can't confirm those numbers, but I wouldn't be surprised if it were 230 days. Or hours, even. War seems as inevitable as death and taxes—with war making those two even more inevitable. The stories in this chapter focus less on the heroes, winners, and losers and more on the overall weirdness that goes on when humans fight.

The Soccer War

Also known as the Football War or the 100-Hours War, this battle was fought by El Salvador and Honduras in July 1969. Tensions were already high between the two countries (border disputes, among other things) when their respective national soccer teams met during a qualifying round for the 1970 World Cup; however, when Honduras beat El Salvador in the Honduran capital on June 8, things went downhill quickly. First, an eighteen-year-old Salvadoran girl, despondent over the loss, shot herself. She quickly became a martyr and the national soccer team even attended her funeral. Then, after two more games, both of which El Salvador won, diplomatic ties were severed and war broke out. After four days, fighting ceased, and though El Salvador gained some concessions from Honduras, their team lost all three games at the World Cup without scoring a goal.

Washington's Gamble

One morning in 1776, British troops in Boston woke up to a surprising sight: Washington's troops and cannons on top of the city's hills preparing to attack. The British counted the cannons and realized they needed to retreat against such a demonstration of firepower. They evacuated the city as quickly as possible and Boston was freed without firing a shot. And it was a good thing for Washington that it went down the way it did, because it was all a total bluff. Sure, Washington's troops had loads of cannons and guns, but they didn't have the gunpowder to use them. If the British had attacked, the patriots would have been able to shoot off a few cannons before running for their lives.

Patton's Stagecraft

By the spring of 1944, Hitler knew Allied Forces were going to create a second front in Europe . . . but where exactly? One good location would be East Anglia and southeast England, where troops could threaten the Port of Calais in France. And that's just what it looked like was happening. General George Patton was there, and so were thousands of troops, tanks, trucks, aircraft, and more. This massive buildup forced Hitler to keep troops stationed at Calais, even as the Allied invasion of Normandy, more than one hundred miles away, began. So what about Patton's massive army? Well, one morning, a British farmer in East Anglia woke up to find a column of American tanks on his land. He noticed one of his bulls size up a tank and then lunge for it. The farmer, expecting a sad end for his bull, was more than surprised when, after impact, the tank started hissing and deflating. All the tanks were fake. So were the aircraft, trucks, and most of the troops. It was all part of Operation Quicksilver—an imaginary army group of set designers, artists, and actors pretending to prepare for attack. The tanks were inflatable rubber, the airplanes were canvas, and the soldiers were made out of wood. Soldiers (real ones) even used rolling tools to create fake tread and tire marks on the dirt roads. Quicksilver was so convincing (including hours and hours of fake, scripted radio traffic) that Hitler kept his panzer divisions in place across from the fake army long after the Allies stormed Normandy on June 6.

Operation Mincemeat

Here's another World War II deception that actually worked. It was 1943 and the Allies were planning to invade Sicily, but wanted the Germans to think they were planning to invade Sardinia and Greece instead. Hmm . . . what to do . . . what to do? Well, the British decided to find a dead body, give it a Royal Marine's uniform, chain a briefcase full of top-secret documents to its wrist, throw it from a submarine off the coast of Spain . . . and then hope for the best. Sure enough, the body washed ashore, the briefcase was opened (they found money, love letters, and a cryptic letter outlining an invasion of either Sardinia or Greece), and the Germans bought it. They pulled thousands of troops from Sicily to defend Sardinia and Greece, and the British parachuted into Sicily.

SIDE NOTE: The British were actually pretty good at this deception business. In North Africa in August 1942, they placed a corpse in a blown-up scout car with a map showing the locations of nonexistent British minefields. The Germans found the map and routed their panzers to a new location where they got bogged down in sand.

A Wing and a Prayer

General George S. Patton and his Third Army were bogged down in Belgium, plagued by rain, flooding, and fog. It was early December 1944, and the Battle of the Bulge was upcoming. Patton, desperate for some good weather, called headquarters and asked if anyone had a good prayer for weather. The man who answered the call, Chaplain James H. O'Neill, wrote a prayer, and under the general's orders had 250,000 copies of the prayer printed and handed out to the whole Third Army.

What happened next during the Battle of the Bulge sounds best coming directly from the chaplain: "On December 20, to the consternation of the Germans and the delight of the American forecasters who were equally surprised at the turnabout, the rains and the fogs ceased. For the better part of a week came bright clear skies and perfect flying weather. Our planes came over by tens, hundreds, and thousands. They knocked out hundreds of tanks, killed thousands of enemy troops in the Bastogne salient, and harried the enemy as he valiantly tried to bring up reinforcements. The 101st Airborne, with the 4th, 9th, and 10th Armored Divisions, which saved Bastogne, and other divisions, which assisted so valiantly in driving the Germans home, will testify to the great support rendered by our air forces. General Patton prayed for fair weather for battle. He got it."

O'Neill received a Bronze Star from Patton for his prayer.

Seeing Double

Lieutenant General Nathan Bedford Forrest of the Confederate Army had surrounded the well-manned and heavily fortified Union earthwork at Athens, Alabama, on August 24, 1864. Forrest sent a demand for surrender, but the Union commander, Colonel Wallace Campbell, refused to acquiesce unless it could be proven that he was up against a superior force. Forrest happily obliged; however, as Campbell reviewed the Confederate troops, Forrest had the men whom Campbell had already counted quietly move to the back of the line to be counted again. Campbell counted nine thousand men and twenty-four cannons. Forrest actually only have around 3,500 men and eight cannons. Campbell surrendered without a fight.

Civil War Math

The Civil War split the United States in two and was fought along many fronts—even in children's textbooks. Young boys and girls going to school in the South learned math from Lemuel Johnson's *An Elementary Arithmetic, Designed for Beginners* textbook. Here are two problems the children had to solve:

➔ A Confederate soldier captured eight Yankees each day for nine days. How many Yankees did he capture in all?

➔ If one Confederate soldier can whip seven Yankees, how many Confederate soldiers can whip forty-nine Yankees?

Not to be outdone, children learning their ABCs on the northern side of things could read from *The Union ABC* (published in 1865), which was printed in red, white, and blue and taught grammar to preschoolers. Like today's alphabet books, it presented a word from each letter in the alphabet. Here's a sample:

> A is America, land of the free. [So far so good.]
>
> B is a Battle, our soldiers did see.
>
> C is a Captain, who led on his men.
>
> N is for Negro, no longer a slave.
>
> T is a Traitor, that was hung on a tree. [Oh, dear.]
>
> U is the Union, our soldiers did save.

Chew on That!

General Hideki Tojo was the Japanese Prime Minister during World War II, and he was the one who ordered the attack on Pearl Harbor on December 7, 1941. After Japan's surrender in 1945, Tojo was soon captured (not before attempting suicide). After recovering from his injuries, he was moved to a prison in Japan where an American dentist, Jack Mallory, was ordered to make him a new set of dentures. Apparently Tojo loved his sweets. The dentist, however, loved his country and secretly engraved a note to Tojo in Morse code on the teeth. The note read: "Remember Pearl Harbor."

At first, Mallory kept his prank a secret, but a friend of his wrote about it in a letter. The story then reached a local radio station, and it wasn't long before *Stars & Stripes* and newspapers around the world carried the story. In order to avoid any further trouble, Mallory visited Tojo once again, borrowed the dentures,

and ground away the message. Tojo was executed for war crimes on November 12, 1948.

The War of the Oaken Bucket

In 1325, soldiers from the Italian city-state of Modena invaded the city-state of Bologna to steal a bucket. The raid was successful, but not without hundreds of Bologna citizen casualties. Bologna declared war and the two city-states fought on and off for twelve years. Bologna never got their bucket back and to this day it's stored in a bell tower in a Modena cathedral.

Rest in Pieces

➜ In 1838, the president of Mexico, General Antonio López de Santa Anna, had to have his leg amputated after being hit by cannon fire. He ordered a full military burial for the leg.

➜ In 1664, Dutch colonist Peter Stuyvesant also had to have his leg amputated after battling the Spanish in the Caribbean. His leg had a proper Christian burial with full military honors.

➜ Confederate general Stonewall Jackson lost his arm in a friendly-fire incident after the Battle of Chancellorsville. If you visit Chancellorsville, Virginia, you can find where his arm was buried. The grave marker says ARM OF STONEWALL JACKSON, MAY 3, 1863.

➔ Here's another story of missing limbs from the Civil War: Union general Daniel Sickles lost his right leg to a cannonball during the Battle of Gettysburg. Instead of burying the leg, however, Sickles preserved the bones and donated them to the Army Medical Museum (now known as the National Museum of Health and Medicine) in Washington, DC. The bones were presented in a small coffin-shaped box along with a card that said, "With the compliments of Major General D.E.S." Sickles was said to have visited his leg bones every year on the anniversary of the amputation. No word if he visited General Henry Barnum's bullet-riddled hip, which also went on display at the museum after Barnum's death.

The Pork and Beans War

British Canada and the United States fought a war during the winter of 1838–1839 over a boundary dispute between Maine and New Brunswick (then a British territory). Troops amassed on both sides of the border, and then . . . nothing. The war got its name from the food troops sat around and ate while waiting for cooler heads to prevail.

The Pig War

The Pork and Beans War wasn't the only unusually named war between the United States and Great Britain over boundary issues in Canada. In another such war, the disputed area was the San Juan Islands, which lie between Vancouver Island and the US mainland.

With both countries claiming and inhabiting the islands, on June 15, 1859, an American farmer named Lyman Cutlar shot and killed a big black pig that had invaded his garden. The pig was owned by Charles Griffin, who worked at Britain's Hudson's Bay Company. Cutlar offered $10 for the pig. Griffin demanded $100, and when Cutlar refused, British authorities threatened to arrest Cutlar. Some accounts attest to this exchange taking place:

Cutlar: "It was eating my potatoes!"

Griffin: "It is up to you to keep your potatoes out of my pig."

Tensions mounted, and before you could say "ham and cheese," nearly five hundred American troops were stationed on the island and ready to face off against five British warships. Neither side was given permission to fire first, so the two armies exchanged many insults, hoping to goad the other side into action. No shots were ever fired, negotiations brought about an agreement to share the island (which is what they were doing in the first place), and the only casualty was the pig. Today, the San Juan Islands belong to the United States.

Out the Window

It's always fascinating to look back and attempt to ascertain the beginning of certain wars. The Thirty Years' War (1618–1648) was one of Europe's bloodiest wars with more than ten million dead (25 percent of the population of central Europe), and its beginnings can be tied to a bunch of guys throwing a bunch of other guys out a window. In May 1618, a group of Protestants, angered over not being allowed to build churches and hence not being allowed to practice their religion, bribed their way into Hradcany Castle where Catholic regents were meeting. Three men were then tossed out a third-story window. According to the Catholics, either angels or the Virgin Mary magically appeared and cushioned their fall. According to the Protestants, the three men lived because they fell in a dry moat that was filled with manure. Either way, the men lived, but the Defenestration (which means throwing someone out a window) of Prague, which started out as a fight between two religions, soon engulfed Bohemia (modern day Czech Republic), Denmark, Germany, Sweden, Poland, Netherlands, and France.

Incidentally, this is known as the *second* Defenestration of Prague. The first happened in 1419. Prague has a thing about enemies and windows, I guess.

Frozen Assets

General Jean-Charles Pichegru was a distinguished French general during the French Revolution. In 1794, Pichegru led his forces in an invasion of the Netherlands. Upon entering Amsterdam, his scouts learned that the Dutch fleet was stationed nearby. This would normally cause great consternation for the general, but for one fact: The entire fleet was frozen in the bay. Pichegru dispatched a cavalry brigade, which simply marched onto the ice and surrounded the entire fleet.

Turning a Blind Eye

Lord Horatio Nelson was an officer for England's Royal Navy in the late 1700s to early 1800s. He's known for many victories, especially during the Napoleonic Wars. He was also known for his valor and bravery—especially since his many battles had taken a personal toll. He was wounded several times over the years and had lost an arm and his sight in one eye. And at the Battle of Copenhagen in 1801, he used his disadvantage to gain a tough victory against the Danish fleet.

With the battle going badly for the British as they advanced into Copenhagen Harbor, Admiral Sir Hyde Parker, who was holding back in case reinforcements were needed, saw how poorly the fight was going and sent a signal to Nelson to withdraw. Nelson was told of the signal and turned to his flag captain and said, "You know, Foley, I have only one eye. I have a right to be blind sometimes." He then raised the telescope to his blind eye and said, "I really do not see the signal." After a costly battle and lengthy truce negotiations, Nelson emerged victorious. And hence was born the expression, "turning a blind eye."

Holy Toledo!

Did you know Ohio and Michigan once went to war? Known as the most bizarre and least deadly altercation on American soil, the Toledo War of 1835 was over a poorly drawn boundary line. The boundary situation was allowed to simmer for a while until Michigan applied for statehood in 1833. After failed negotiations with Ohio governor Robert Lucas, the nineteen-year-old, hot-headed, territorial governor of Michigan, Stephens T. Mason, sent militia to the contested boundary. Lucas did the same, and it seemed a major battle would ensue. Except for one thing: Both armies got lost in the swamps at the boundary, and for one week simply couldn't find each other. The dispute was resolved in 1836. Michigan lost Toledo, but gained statehood. Plus, Congress gave them the Upper Peninsula, which, in retrospect, is a much better piece of land than Toledo.

Ironic Elephants

John Sedgwick is known more for his famous last words than for any of his exploits as a Union general during the Civil War. At the beginning of the Battle of Spotsylvania Court House in 1864, Sedgwick and his troops were scouting artillery placements while Confederate sharpshooters about a thousand yards away were taking pot shots. While members of his staff flinched at the sound of shots, Sedgwick said, "What? Men dodging this way for single bullets? What will you do when they open fire along the whole line? I am ashamed of you. They couldn't hit an elephant at this distance." When his men continued flinching, Sedgwick continued, "I'm ashamed of you, dodging that way. They couldn't hit an elephant at this distan—" They could, though, and Sedgwick died of a bullet wound below his left eye.

The 335 Years' War

Known as one of the world's longest wars, the 335 Years' War was between the Netherlands and the Isles of Scilly (located off the southwest coast of the United Kingdom). Two points of interest here: No shots were ever fired, and a peace treaty was finally signed in 1986. The ambassador to the Dutch Embassy in London joked that it must have been scary to the Scillonians "to know we could have attacked at any moment."

The Great Emu War

In 1932, Australia declared war against a bird. Or to be more precise, they declared war against twenty thousand or more emus (think ostrich but a tad shorter). Farmers in Western Australia were complaining about the great number of emus, which were moving into settled areas and destroying crops because of drought and food shortages. A military operation under the command of Major Meredith of the Royal Australian Artillery was undertaken in November. He, along with two soldiers with machine guns and ten thousand rounds of ammunition, set out to engage the emus, but it wasn't as easy as it sounded. The emus ran away at the sound of gunfire, and even the few that the soldiers were able to hit simply ran off. Ornithologist Dominic Serventy put it this way: "The machine gunner's dreams of point-blank fire into the serried masses of emus were soon dissipated. The emu command had evidently ordered guerilla tactics, and its unwieldy army soon split into innumerable small units that made use of the military equipment uneconomic."

After a few days, the Defense Minister ordered a complete withdrawal. The emus had won.

The Original Foo Fighters

Although most people would say that the Foo Fighters is a rock band, the term actually goes back to World War II. During the war, many Allied pilots reported seeing mysterious orbs of light that would follow them on their missions and keep pace with each maneuver. These flying objects were spotted both in the Pacific and European theaters of operation and appeared from 1941 until the end of the war. Eyewitness accounts describe these lights as "a strange globe glowing with greenish light," "a large cylindrical object that traveled thousands of miles per hour," "two fog lights flying at high rates of speed that could change direction rapidly," and more. Allied pilots began calling these glowing balls Foo Fighters (*foo* was a popular nonsense word at the time and the terms flying saucer and UFO weren't used yet). The Foo Fighters never attacked, and at times seemed almost playful in their ability to keep pace with the planes and then suddenly shoot off into the sky. After the first sightings, Allied forces investigated whether or not these lights were some sort of secret German weapon. They soon learned, however, that Japanese and German pilots also reported seeing the same weird glowing balls. Were Foo Fighters optical illusions, electrostatic discharges, ball lightning . . . or aliens watching the humans destroy one another? No satisfactory explanation has ever been offered.

Sticky Bomb

During World War II, the British, in dire need of a weapon to combat tanks (due to their lack of antitank guns), came up with the Anti-Tank No. 74, also known as the sticky bomb. It was actually a hand grenade that consisted of a glass sphere containing nitroglycerin. The sphere was covered in a strong adhesive and surrounded by a metal casing. The user simply had to pull the pin to remove the casing and then throw or place the grenade, which would stick to the enemy tank. Sounds reasonable, yes? Home Guard member Bill Miles recounted an unexpected problem with the grenade: "It was while practicing that an HG bomber got his stick(y) bomb stuck to his trouser leg and couldn't shift it. A quick-thinking mate whipped the trousers off and got rid of them and the bomb. After the following explosion the trousers were in a bit of a mess, though I think they were in a bit of a mess prior to the explosion."

Belle of the War

Maria "Belle" Boyd was a seventeen-year-old debutante in 1861, when an incident at her house in Front Royal, Virginia, turned her into one of the best-known spies of the Civil War.

Rumors abounded that her home was flying one or more Confederate flags. A few drunk Union soldiers went to check it out.

Belle's mother got angry and one of the soldiers pushed her aside to get to a flag. At that point, Belle interjected her own opinion into the matter by pulling out a pistol and shooting the pushy soldier to death. She was exonerated (her actions were declared self-defense), but sentries were posted around the house. She charmed one of the sentries into revealing military secrets. She later wrote, "To him I am indebted for some very remarkable effusions, some withered flowers, and last, but not least, for a great deal of important information . . . I must avow the flowers and the poetry were comparatively valueless in my eyes." Belle made sure those secrets got into the right Confederate hands, and a spy was born.

One of her more famous excursions occurred in May 1862. Upon hearing that a Union general and his staff were gathering at a local hotel, Boyd hid herself in the room just above where they were meeting and listened in through a knothole in the floor that she may have enlarged earlier in the day. She learned that part of the Union army was heading east, leaving their position at Front Royal weak. She relayed this information, and when the Confederate army attacked a few days later, Boyd ran across enemy lines to greet Stonewall Jackson's army, yelling, "The Yankee force is very small. Tell him to charge right down and he will catch them all!" That's just what Jackson did, and that very evening he sent her a note that said, "I thank you, for myself and for the army, for the immense service that you have rendered your country today." She was also awarded the Southern Cross of Honor and made both a captain and an honorary aide-de-camp. Another memento of her bravery that day was the skirt she wore, which was now filled with bullet holes from her dangerous jaunt.

She continued spying, even though she was captured and imprisoned three separate times. (The first time her boyfriend turned her in.) She sailed for Britain in 1864, supposedly to deliver some letters from Jackson. The ship was captured by the Union Navy, but she was allowed to escape by a Union sailor named Lieutenant Samuel Hardinge. He had fallen in love with her, and they later met up in Britain and married. Boyd gained much fame as a spy. French newspapers called her "la Belle Rebelle," and Boyd used her notoriety to get into acting.

The Turkey Tactic

Alvin Cullum York was born in 1887 in a log cabin in Pall Mall, Tennessee. A wild youth and expert shot, he converted to Christianity after a friend was killed in a bar fight. He joined a church that forbade violence, and when he was drafted in 1917 for World War I, he wrote on his draft notice, "Don't want to fight." Yet fight he did.

He was sent overseas, and during a battle in the Argonne Forest in France, he and sixteen other soldiers were sent behind German lines to capture machine gun positions and a rail line. They captured a bunch of German soldiers eating breakfast, but then the machine guns turned around and started shooting at them. Six of York's comrades were killed and two were wounded, and York found himself in charge. York, reminded of the turkey shoots back home, "began to exchange shots with them. In order to sight me or to swing their machine guns on me, the Germans had to show their heads above the trench, and every time I saw a head I just touched it off." Growing up, York had learned that the best way to hunt geese was to shoot the birds in the back of the row first so the others didn't scatter. He did the same thing when a group of six Germans rushed at him—knocking off the ones in the back before shooting the ones up front.

The Germans had seen enough and surrendered. York and the seven remaining Americans had more than eighty prisoners on their hands, but they were still behind enemy lines. York put a German major at the head of the line of prisoners, held a gun on him, and began to escort them back to the American side. By the time they got there, they had more than 130 prisoners. It was determined that York had single-handedly killed twenty-eight Germans.

He received the Congressional Medal of Honor and the Distinguished Service Cross, as well as France's Croix de Guerre and Legion of Honor. The Supreme Allied Commander said, "What York did was the greatest thing accomplished by any soldier of all the armies of Europe." York was played by Gary Cooper in a movie about his heroic deeds.

Public Relations 101

Pharaoh Ramses II (aka Ozymandias) was soundly defeated by the Hittites at the Battle of Kedesh in 1288 BCE. Afterward, Ramses built a memorial to his amazing triumph. Huh? That's right, Ramses II returned to his empire and declared victory, even though he was ambushed by the Hittites and forced to retreat. The Hittites are gone. All eyewitnesses are gone. Ramses's memorials

to his "victory" remain, and it has only recently been unearthed by archaeologists that Ramses was fibbing.

The Drunken War

After the fall of the Soviet Union, the Republic of Moldova (located between Romania and Ukraine) declared itself an independent state. It sought closer ties with Romania, but the area of the country closest to Russia and Ukraine broke away in 1990 and named itself Transnistria. The two sides battled on and off from March till July 1992, when a ceasefire was declared. But it seems there were plenty of ceasefires every evening—when combatants on both sides of the conflict would put down their weapons to drink together.

Yankee Doodle Diddy

The song "Yankee Doodle Dandy" was written by a British surgeon during the French and Indian War to ridicule the colonial militiamen who were fighting alongside British soldiers. As the American Revolution drew near, the song became a popular insult the British soldiers used—often making up new verses that mocked the colonists.

On April 19, 1775, as British troops marched toward Lexington and Concord, Redcoats played the song on fife and drum and sang it heartily. However, as rebels battled with the British, eventually turning them back, the Redcoats were surprised to hear the colonists singing "Yankee Doodle." One British soldier later said, "Damn them, they made us dance it till we were tired."

From that moment on, the colonists sang the song in battle, taking delight in the self-mockery. They even played it while the British surrendered at Saratoga and Yorktown. British Lieutenant Thomas Anburey wrote: ". . . the name [Yankee] has been more prevalent since the commencement of hostilities . . . The soldiers at Boston used it as a term of reproach, but after the affair at Bunker's Hill, the Americans gloried in it. Yankee Doodle is now their paean, a favorite of favorites, played in their army, esteemed as warlike as the Genadier's March—it is the lover's spell, the nurse's lullaby . . . it was not a little mortifying to hear them play this tune, when their army marched down to our surrender."

SIDE NOTE: The term *Yankee* may have come from the Dutch word *jahnke*, which was used to describe an uncultured person. The word *doodle* referred to uneducated farmers and backwoodsmen—hicks. Meanwhile, *macaroni* referred to certain young foppish British men and women who at the time wore outlandish clothing and spoke Italian in an affected way to show that they were cultured. They were called *Macaronies*.

An Army of Two

During the War of 1812, Abigail and Rebecca Bates, daughter of Captain Simeon Bates, prevented an attack by the British on their town. Their father was the keeper of the lighthouse in Scituate, Massachusetts, a fishing village about thirty miles from Boston. During the summer of 1814, the girls saw two barges from a British ship filled with soldiers. With no time to call an alarm, the girls grabbed a fife and drum from the lighthouse, hid behind some trees, and began playing "Yankee Doodle Dandy" as loudly as possible. The British thought the sounds were coming from a regiment of American soldiers and retreated.

The Luckiest Man Alive

In 1918, during a World War I dogfight, British flying ace Reginald Makepeace of the No. 20 Squadron went into a steep dive to dodge German gunfire. Captain J. H. Hedley, who was in the back seat of the cockpit, was thrown from the plane. As the plane leveled off several hundred feet below, Hedley landed on the tail of the plane and hung on for dear life as the plane landed safely.

Calvin's Ruse

In 1942, Calvin Graham enlisted in the US Navy. He was quickly shipped out to the Pacific, where he joined the crew of the USS *South Dakota* as a gunner. During the Battle of Guadalcanal, he was seriously wounded while helping fight a fire aboard the ship. For all his efforts, he was dishonorably discharged, stripped of his medals, and put in the brig. Why? After he received the Bronze Star and the Purple Heart, Calvin's mother revealed Calvin's secret: he was only twelve years old. After a couple of months in the brig, Calvin went back to seventh grade. He spent much of his adult life trying to clear his record and get his medals and disability benefits back.

He was finally awarded an honorable discharge in 1978 and he received disability and back pay in 1988. Rick Schroder played him in a TV movie of his life.

Ask, Tell

Let's travel back to 371 BCE and the Battle of Leuctra. The famed Spartan army was defeated by armies of the city-state Thebes—effectively ending Sparta's dominance over Greece. The key point of the battle came when an elite Theban unit known as the Sacred Band led a breakthrough against Spartan defenses. These three hundred soldiers were fierce, brave, committed . . . and gay. The unit was composed of 150 gay couples, and the thinking of the band's organizer, Gorgidas, was that each man would fight his best to protect his lover, who was fighting alongside him. The band remained undefeated for more than thirty years, until, surrounded by Macedonian forces, they fought to the death (while other Theban troops retreated). A giant stone lion resides at the burial site of the Sacred Band in the town of Thebes.

Weapons of Mass Destruction, Old School–Style

Archimedes, master mathematician, inventor, and all-around genius, nearly single-handedly fended off a powerful Roman force that was attacking the city of Syracuse in 213 BCE. Although the Roman fleet commanded by Marcus Claudius Marcellus was impressive, their siege, which had been estimated to take a week, lasted nearly two years. As military advisor to the king of Syracuse, Archimedes developed several weapons that helped keep the Romans at bay. One such weapon consisted of several mirrors, which Archimedes used to direct the sun's rays onto the Romans' ships, setting them ablaze. Other inventions included catapults that could hurl a ton of stones onto the ships, mousetrap-like mechanisms that sent rocks down onto siege ladders, and a giant grappling claw, called the Claw of Archimedes, which lifted ships by the bow and dropped them against the rocks, sinking them. The Romans finally succeeded in breaching the city's defenses, and although General Marcellus ordered Archimedes not to be harmed, a Roman soldier killed him.

General Buck Naked

During the First Liberian War in 1992, General Joshua Milton Blahyi would lead his troops wearing only his shoes. He says the devil telephoned him at age eleven and told him that running into battle naked would make him impervious to bullets. Sometimes he and his soldiers would also don colorful wigs and dainty purses. He's still alive, so I guess it worked. The devil also said it would be a good idea to practice human sacrifice and cannibalism to increase his power. Blahyi admits to sacrificing a small child or teenager before battles, including sometimes cutting out the heart and eating it. Today he is the president of the End Time Train Evangelistic Ministries, and he has repented his sins, blamed the devil for his actions, and expressed a willingness to be tried for war crimes.

Battle Fatigue

→ The British had actually buckled to demands and lowered tea taxes before the Boston Tea Party.

→ An OSS staff psychologist came up with an ingenious (or idiotic) plan during World War II that he believed would send an already unhinged Hitler over the edge. He theorized that Hitler would suffer a mental breakdown if tons of pornography were dropped in and around his home. The Royal Air Force refused to carry out the plan.

→ At the start of the Civil War, Confederate Robert E. Lee owned no slaves. Union general Ulysses S. Grant did.

→ Spain declared war against the United States on April 24, 1898. The United States then had the date of its own declaration set at April 21, even though they actually declared war on April 25.

→ Henry Kissinger and Yassir Arafat won the Nobel Peace Prize. Gandhi didn't.

→ The shortest war on record was fought between the United Kingdom and Zanzibar on August 27, 1896. It lasted around forty minutes, with Britain whipping the Zanzibaris with a massive bombardment that disabled Zanzibar's defenses.

→ The *D* in *D-Day* doesn't stand for *deliverance*, *doom*, or even *debarkation*. It doesn't stand for anything. The *D* is derived from the word *day*, and the term *D-Day*, (or *Day-Day*) was used for many different operations, even if it's only remembered today as the name for the invasion of Normandy.

→ Arlington National Cemetery, the military cemetery for US armed forces, was established during the Civil War on land "appropriated" from Robert E. Lee, commanding general of the Confederate army.

→ "Dixie," the unofficial anthem of the South during the Civil War, was written in 1859 by Daniel Decatur Emmett, a northerner who was loyal to the Union.

HISTORICAL MOMENTS

"History is always written wrong, and so always needs to be rewritten."—George Santayana

Right after a historic moment, we revel in the details. We want to know everything that happened and how it went down and who was there. As years pass, these moments get chopped down into one-sentence sidebars in textbooks. This chapter seeks to correct this injustice with stories about insignificant or just plain weird moments from history's footnotes, what-ifs, and greatest hits.

Dead End

The assassination of Archduke Franz Ferdinand, heir to the throne of the Austro-Hungarian Empire, was a pivotal point in history—sending several countries into a war that would become known as World War I. Perhaps all of that war nonsense could have been avoided if Ferdinand's driver hadn't made a wrong turn.

On June 28, 1914, Ferdinand and his wife were in a motorcade in Sarajevo, Bosnia, where tensions were high and Ferdinand wasn't very popular. At one point a bomb was thrown at his open-topped car. It bounced off and detonated behind them. Ferdinand is known to have shouted, "So, you welcome your guests with bombs!" Later, while either attempting to rush out of the city or to visit those injured in the blast earlier in the day, his driver made a wrong turn and began backing up right near one of the conspirators, Gavilo Princip, a nineteen-year-old Slavic Nationalist. While the car slowly backed up not five feet away, and with a second chance just fallen into his lap, Princip drew his pistol and shot the Archduke and his wife.

SIDE NOTE: If you don't like the idea of blaming a wrong turn for the start of World War I, consider this: The Archduke was such a perfectionist about the cut and fit of his military uniform that he had a one-piece garment sewn on to him each day. So when doctors attempted to examine his wounds after he was shot, they realized the buttons didn't work, and by the time they figured out they had to cut the uniform off, the Archduke was dead.

Suffering Suffrage

The US Congress passed and ratified the Nineteenth Amendment in 1920, giving women the right to vote. But before that, some women did have the right to vote in elections. After the American Revolution, women in New Jersey could vote until 1807. And, before Utah was granted statehood, women were given the right to vote (without even really asking for it) expressly to help make polygamy illegal, which would then make Utah a more desirable candidate for US statehood. Once polygamy was finally outlawed, women lost the right to vote once again . . . presumably to make Utah a more desirable candidate for US statehood.

SIDE NOTE: Two women, Victoria Woodhull and Belva Ann Lockwood ran for president of the United States before 1920, even though, under law, they couldn't vote for themselves.

Listen to Mother

Today we take for granted women's right to vote; however, the vote in Congress that fateful day in 1920 was too close for comfort. Thirty-six of forty-eight states were needed to ratify, and the Nineteenth Amendment was one vote shy. Its only hope was Harry Burn, a Republican from Tennessee. He was firmly in the "no way" camp until receiving a letter from his mother. It said, "Don't forget to be a good boy and help Mrs. Catt put the 'rat' in ratification. Signed, your mother." He changed his vote and later explained, "I know that a mother's advice is always safest for her boy to follow, and my mother wanted me to vote for ratification." Bet you he got an extra cookie in his lunch after that!

United States of France?

Napoleon had big plans for the vast territory that France held in North America. In 1802 he sent an army to take control of New Orleans and open the doors for a new wave of French colonists to populate a New France. The army's first stop, however, was Haiti. There, troops were ordered to reestablish French rule after a slave rebellion. While the Haitians were no match for French troops, something far more menacing attacked: mosquitoes. More specifically, mosquitoes carrying yellow fever. Of the original twenty thousand troops sent, only a few thousand lived. Napoleon responded by sending reinforcements. Thousands more perished—up to fifty thousand troops by some estimates. Meanwhile, the largely immune local population renewed the fight with guerilla-type attacks. The few living French soldiers soon surrendered and returned to France. With most of his expeditionary force completely destroyed, Napoleon gave up on his dream of a New France and sold his empire of the Mississippi Valley to the United States

Notes on the Declaration of Independence

On July 4, 1776, the Continental Congress, meeting in the Pennsylvania State House in Philadelphia, approved the Declaration of Independence. There are lots of fun stories about the Declaration, although many of them are in dispute or outright incorrect. (For example, Ben Franklin did not add to an early version of the document, "kiss our collective arse.") Let's set the record straight:

→ The Declaration of Independence is the document that severed the colonies' ties to the British Crown and set in motion the American Revolution . . . right? Well, yes, but it was meant more as a press release for the colonists since the Lee Resolution (aka the Resolution of Independence), which was passed on July 2, 1776, declared the United Colonies to be independent of the British. John Adams even thought July 2 would be the day future Americans celebrated. He wrote to his wife: "The second day of July, 1776, will be the most memorable epoch in the history of America. I am apt to believe that it will be celebrated by succeeding generations as the great anniversary festival . . . It ought to be celebrated with pomp and parade, with shows, games, sports, guns, bells, bonfires, and illuminations . . ." Well, at least he got the pomp and parades right.

→ Who exactly signed the Declaration, and when? Historians still argue over this. Most say it was actually signed on August 2, 1776, and not on July 4, even though Thomas Jefferson, Ben Franklin, and John Adams all wrote that it was signed on July 4. In 1796, one of the signers disputed this by pointing out that some of the signers weren't even in Philadelphia on July 4—including some who weren't even elected to Congress at that time. These days, it's thought most signed the Declaration in August.

→ Thomas Jefferson loved telling people that the final vote on the Declaration was approved quickly because a swarm of flies from a nearby stable invaded the session, forcing a quick vote. Other stories state Jefferson actually complained about the flies at the Graff House, where he wrote the Declaration.

→ Richard Stockton of New Jersey, one of the original signers of the Declaration, violated his oath to his new nation when he was taken prisoner and tortured by the British. He was starved and left exposed to freezing temperatures before being let go after signing an oath swearing allegiance to George III.

→ The most famous version of the Declaration of Independence is a handwritten copy that's signed by all the delegates. It's generally regarded as the official document, and it's the one on display at the National Archives in Washington, DC. It's important to note that this wasn't the original document.

→ The Dunlap broadsides were the first published copies of the Declaration of Independence. They were printed on July 4, 1776, and around two hundred were printed. Only twenty-six are known to survive. In 1989, a flea-market bargain hunter found one inside a framed painting he bought for $4.00. It was sold for more than $8 million.

→ The original handwritten Declaration (signed by John Hancock as president of the Continental Congress) was used by the printer to set type to print copies. It hasn't been seen since.

→ What's really written on the back of the Declaration of Independence? No, it's not a secret code like in the movie *National Treasure*. It says, "Original Declaration of Independence, dated 4th July 1776." Nobody knows who wrote it.

→ Jefferson's first draft of the Declaration had an antislavery paragraph in it that was deleted so South Carolina and Georgia would approve it.

→ Actor Reese Witherspoon claims to be a descendant of John Witherspoon, a signatory of the Declaration.

Return to Sender

The historic flight of the *Friendship 7* was the first to put an American in orbit. The lucky American was John Glenn. Upon learning that it may take up to three days to retrieve him after landing back on earth, and that the likely landing sites were Australia, New Guinea, and the ocean, Glenn became worried about a hostile response from aborigine populations he might encounter. Think about it. You're sitting there, minding your own business, when suddenly a metal contraption comes from the sky, lands on your hut, and from it emerges a shiny silver creature. Glenn had the following message translated into several languages:

I am a stranger. I come in peace. Take me to your leader, and there will be a massive reward for you in eternity.

Party Crashers

It would be rare for you or me to be invited to a presidential inauguration party at the White House—we're just regular people. Andrew Jackson, however, thought that since regular people voted for him, they should be invited to the party. So, after the swearing in, thousands followed him back to the White House. I'll let Margaret Bayard Smith take it from here (from Smith's *The First Forty Years of Washington Society*): "But what a scene did we witness . . . The President, after having been literally nearly pressed to death and almost suffocated and torn to pieces by the people in their eagerness to shake hands with Old Hickory, had retreated through the back way or south front and had escaped to his lodgings at Gadsby's . . . Cut glass and china to the amount of several thousand dollars had been broken in the struggle to get the refreshments . . . Ladies fainted, men were seen with bloody noses, and such a scene of confusion took place as is impossible to describe—those who got in could not get out by the door again, but had to scramble out of windows."

A few ingenious waiters decided to place giant tubs of punch on the White House lawn. Once lured outside, the rabble was locked out. The White House suffered thousands of dollars worth of damage. No one can say Jackson didn't earn his moniker, King Mob, honestly.

You'll Catch Your Death

When William Harrison became president in 1840, he ran on his reputation as the hero of the Battle of Tippecanoe. Seeking to prove he still had it, he took the oath of office on March 4, 1841, a cold and rainy day. Wearing neither a coat nor a hat, he proceeded to deliver the longest inaugural address in American history. It took him two hours to read it. Soon after, he caught a cold that turned into pneumonia and pleurisy. He was dead thirty days after becoming president. Today, medical professionals agree that exposure to the elements doesn't cause respiratory illnesses; however, the common perception remains that Harrison died because he didn't wear a coat at his inauguration.

Village Idiots

On June 4, 1783, the Montgolfier brothers, inventors of the first hot-air balloon, demonstrated their invention to a crowd at the market square in the French village of Annonay. A bonfire fed the tethered thirty-three–foot taffeta contraption, and then one of the brothers cut the tether and set the balloon free. It traveled six thousand feet into the air before landing in a field several miles away . . . where it was attacked by peasants with pitchforks, who thought it was a beast from the sky come down to attack them. They tore the balloon to pieces and tied it to the tail of a horse.

Stupid Predictions

➔ "Four or five frigates will do the business without any military force."—British Prime Minister Lord Frederick North, on dealing with those pesky rebellious American colonies, 1774

➔ "The automobile will never, of course, come into as common use as the bicycle."—*Literary Digest*, 1899

→ "Who the hell wants to hear actors talk?"—H. M. Warner, head of Warner Bros. Studios, 1927

→ "I see no good reason why the views given in this volume should shock the religious feelings of any one."—Charles Darwin, in *The Origin of Species*, 1869

→ "Stocks have reached what looks like a permanently high plateau."—Economist Irving Fisher, 1929

→ "It will be gone by June."—*Variety* magazine on rock and roll, 1955

→ "Displays no trace of imagination, good taste or ingenuity. I say it's a stinkeroo."—Film critic Russell Maloney on *The Wizard of Oz*, 1939

→ "There are not enough Indians in the world to defeat the Seventh Cavalry."—General George Custer, 1876

→ "If anything remains more or less unchanged, it will be the role of women."—David Riesman, social scientist, 1967

→ "It's a great invention but who would want to use it anyway?" —Rutherford B. Hayes, after a demonstration of Alexander Graham Bell's telephone, 1876

→ "A rocket will never be able to leave the Earth's atmosphere." —*The New York Times*, 1936

➔ "The cinema is little more than a fad. It's canned drama. What audiences really want to see is flesh and blood on the stage." —Charlie Chaplin, 1916

➔ "The problem with television is that the people must sit and keep their eyes glued on a screen; the average American family hasn't time for it."—*The New York Times*, 1939

➔ "So many centuries after the Creation it is unlikely that anyone could find hitherto unknown lands of any value."—Committee advising King Ferdinand and Queen Isabella regarding proposal by Christopher Columbus, 1486

➔ "There is no reason for any individual to have a computer in his home."—Ken Olsen, founder of Digital Equipment Corporation, 1977

Putting on Hairs

Nearly anyone who thinks about Abraham Lincoln pictures him with a beard, which is interesting since he went beardless nearly all his life. However, while campaigning as the Republican nominee for president in 1860, Lincoln received some fashion advice in a letter from an eleven-year-old girl named Grace Bedell. She wrote, "I have got 4 brothers, and part of them will vote for you any way and if you will let your whiskers grow I will try and get the rest of them to vote for you. You would look a great deal better for your face is so thin. All the ladies like whiskers and they would tease their husbands to vote for you and then you would be President." Lincoln took her advice and won the presidency. During his trip to the White House in 1861, he met up with the young letter writer and said, "You see, Grace, I let my whiskers grow for you." Who knows what would have happened if Grace had never written to Lincoln?

Lincoln's Last Laugh

On April 14, 1865, Lincoln and his wife, Mary, attended the play *Our American Cousin* at Ford's Theatre. Mary had complained of a headache and was thinking of not going. Lincoln, feeling a little tired himself, decided they should go because he said he needed a laugh. Before leaving for the theater, he had pronounced it the happiest day in his life. The Civil War was over, and he had just given Secretary Stanton the order to end the draft. During the play, actor Edward Sothern appeared onstage with the heroine, who had a shawl over her shoulder. She said, "Me lord, will you kindly throw my shawl over my shoulders—there appears to be a draft here?" Sothern, glancing directly at Lincoln gave this impromptu line: "You are mistaken, Miss Mary, the draft has already been stopped by order of the President!" Lincoln joined the audience in what ended up being his last laugh.

Have a Cigar

During the Civil War, on September 13, 1862, General George Mc-Clellan and his Union troops were moving to intercept Robert E. Lee's forces in Maryland. They stopped at a campsite where Lee's army had stayed a few days earlier. Two soldiers relaxing on the ground found three cigars wrapped in a piece of paper. Right before tossing the paper and sharing the cigars, Corporal Barton W. Mitchell decided to take a look at the wrapping. And good thing he did, for on it was written Lee's battle plans, including the fact that Lee had divided his army in order to attack near Antietam Creek. It turned into a bad day for the Confederates as they were beaten at the Battle of Sharpsburg in what was the single bloodiest day of combat in American history. Incredibly, even though McClellan said, "Here is a paper with which if I cannot whip Bobby Lee I will be willing to go home," things would have gone even worse for Lee if McClellan hadn't waited *nearly a full day* before deciding to take advantage of the found information.

NOTE: McClellan wasn't known as the most aggressive general of the Civil War. In fact, at times "Young Napoleon" was criticized for being downright passive. In 1862, Abraham Lincoln said of McClellan, "If General McClellan isn't going to use his army, I'd like to borrow it for a time."

Hound Bites

Henry VIII, he of the six wives, didn't set out to start his own church. In fact, when he wanted to annul his marriage to his first wife, Catherine of Aragon, he sent Cardinal Thomas Wolsey, one of his most important government ministers, to appeal to the Pope. All was going well, and Wolsey had the annulment in hand, when he kneeled to kiss the Pope's toe. Unfortunately, Wolsey's greyhound,

Urian, who for some reason was in attendance, ran up and bit the Pope's foot. The Pope ended negotiations and refused to grant the annulment. The English Reformation soon followed.

Freedom at Any Cost

Henry Brown was a slave in Virginia who, despondent over his wife and children being sold to a slave trader, decided to seek freedom any way he could. Along with the help of Samuel Smith, a white shopkeeper sympathetic to his cause, Brown devised an ingenious escape. He mailed his way to freedom. Brown paid $86 to have himself shipped to Philadelphia abolitionist James Miller McKim. On March 23, 1849, Brown had himself packed into a 3 x 2 x 2.6 box (hopefully labeled "This Side Up/Handle with Care") with a bottle of water. He was loaded onto a wagon, and then a train . . . a steamboat . . . another wagon . . . another train . . . and finally, the delivery wagon, which dropped him off at McKim's residence approximately twenty-seven hours later.

Brown went on to have a successful career as a speaker for the Anti-Slavery Society and was given the not-so-clever nickname "Box" at a Boston antislavery convention in 1849. Outrage over his and other slaves' escape stories led to the Fugitive Slave Act of 1850, which declared that all runaway slaves must be brought back to their owners. This forced Brown to move to England, where he toured an antislavery panorama he called "Mirror of Slavery" for ten years. He returned to the United States after the Civil War in 1875 with a family magic act. (He had remarried while in England.)

SIDE NOTE: In 1914, four-year-old May Pierstorff of Grangeville, Idaho, was to visit her grandmother in Lewiston. Her parents, figuring it was cheaper to mail her than to put her on a train, pinned fifty-three cents to the young girl's coat (they were charged the chicken rate—it was legal to mail chickens back then) and handed her to the mailman. May traveled the entire distance in the train's mail compartment and was delivered safely to her grandmother by the mail clerk on duty. It took another six years after this for mailing your kid to be considered illegal.

Houston, We Hate the Number Thirteen

Here's one for the "What in the world were they thinking?" category. Sure, scientists are supposed to be objective, and you can forgive them for not being superstitious about black cats and knocking on wood. However, *Apollo 13*, the ill-fated lunar launch, was the thirteenth scheduled lunar space exploration mission, scheduled for liftoff at the thirteenth minute after the thirteenth hour, with the lunar landing scheduled for the thirteenth day of April. Come on! That's just asking for trouble. When did things go all to hell? On the thirteenth.

E Pluribus Yum Yum

The Latin phrase *E pluribus unum* (out of many, one) was adopted by Benjamin Franklin, John Adams, and Thomas Jefferson as the motto for the Second Continental Congress. It was also later chosen to grace the Seal of the United States. At the time of the American Revolution, this exact phrase appeared on the title page of a popular magazine, *The Gentleman's Magazine*. The phrase is attributed to Virgil, the Roman poet. The poem in which the phrase appeared was about . . . salad, and the phrase describes the blending of colors into one.

Strange but True

→ President Lincoln was the first president to be photographed at his inauguration. The photo was taken at his second inauguration in 1865. In the photo, John Wilkes Booth can be seen standing close to Lincoln.

→ In 1859, the United States minted a new coin, which has just about always been known as the Indian-head penny. Unfortunately, there's no Indian on it. The engraver, James B. Longacre, modeled Lady Liberty wearing a "feather bonnet."

→ Thomas Jefferson once introduced a compromise bill in Congress that would have barred slavery in all future states admitted to the Union. It could very well have prevented the Civil War; unfortunately, it was defeated by a single vote.

→ Strange? Yes. True? I hope so. In April 1939, Japanese Prime Minister Fumimaro Konoye's hemorrhoids kept him from attending an important Cabinet meeting with his Minister of Foreign Affairs, which led to a misunderstanding about a US peace proposal that may have contributed to Japan's entry into World War II.

→ British POWs in World War II were allowed care packages, and in many of these packages were games of Monopoly with secret silk maps hidden between the boards of the game, real money, a small compass, and even some tiny files.

→ Junius Booth, father of John Wilkes Booth, sent a death threat to President Andrew Jackson in 1835.

It's Witchcraft

The whole Salem, Massachusetts, witch fiasco of 1692 (where more than 150 people were arrested, nineteen were hanged, and one man was crushed to death under heavy stones) wasn't the only witch activity during colonial times in the United States. Where Salem quickly dissolved into one of the most famous cases of mass hysteria, in other colonies, cooler heads usually prevailed.

Pennsylvania only had one witch trial, and it occurred on December 27, 1683. Two old Swedish women had been accused of witchcraft, but it seems only one stood trial. The proof against Margaret Mattson, known as the Witch of Ridley Creek, was circumstantial to say the least. The first witness testified that he heard that twenty years ago Mattson bewitched several cows. Another witness reported that his mother told him Mattson had bewitched her cow. A third also talked of bewitched animals, although he also threw in a story about a friend's wife being threatened by an apparition sent by the accused.

Thankfully, William Penn, founder of Pennsylvania and the Attorney General, presided. His intelligence and sense of fairness prevailed, especially when, because of some confusion (Mattson didn't speak English), Mattson confessed to being a witch. Penn asked her, "Art thou a witch? Hast thou ridden through the air on a broomstick?" Mattson said, "Yes." Some accounts of this event say that, thinking quickly, Penn announced that there was no law against riding on broomsticks, and he ordered her discharged. But because of the confession, the jury came back with this ruling: "Guilty of having the Common Fame of a Witch, but not Guilty in manner and Forme as Shee stands Endicted." (The jury should have been found guilty of gross misuse of the English language.) In other words, she was guilty of being called a witch but not guilty of actually being one. She was released on bail.

Poor Eyesight Saves the Day

Two-time president Theodore Roosevelt decided in 1912 that he wasn't done with national politics, so he challenged his successor, William Howard Taft, for their party's nomination. On October 14, 1912, as Roosevelt was about to step into a car that would take him to a campaign rally in Milwaukee, Wisconsin, John F. Schrank went up to him and shot him in the chest at point-blank range. Now, because of a boxing injury, Roosevelt's eyesight was poor, so he usually wrote his speeches on small sheets of paper with large words and spaces to help him see it better. Hence, his speech manuscripts were often quite thick, and the speech he was to give that day saved his life. The bullet passed through the speech as well as his steel eyeglasses case (both of which were in Roosevelt's coat pocket) before lodging in his chest. Without the speech impeding the bullet's progress, the missile would have hit his heart. Undaunted, Roosevelt continued on to the rally and gave his ninety-minute speech in his bloody clothes. He began his speech thusly: "Friends, I shall ask you to be as quiet as possible. I don't know whether you fully understand that I have just been shot; but it takes more than that to kill a Bull Moose. But fortunately I had my manuscript, so you see I was going to make a long speech, and there is a bullet—there is where the bullet went through—and it probably saved me from it going into my heart. The bullet is in me now, so that I cannot make a very long speech, but I will try my best."

After a short convalescence, Roosevelt resumed his campaign. He lost the nomination to Taft, but ran as part of the brand-new Bull Moose Party. Taft and Roosevelt both lost in a four-way contest to Woodrow Wilson.

Booth Saves Lincoln's Life

Okay, not *that* Booth and not *that* Lincoln. In an interesting coincidence of history, Abraham Lincoln's son Robert was once saved from serious injury by John Wilkes Booth's brother, Edwin.

Edwin was an actor like his brother; however, while John was known as a competent-if-not-inspired actor, Edwin was perhaps the finest Shakespearean actor of the nineteenth century. The two brothers were not close. Edwin was a Unionist and staunch Lincoln supporter. When he told his brother he had voted for Lincoln's reelection, Edwin wrote, "He expressed deep regret, and declared his belief that Lincoln would be made king of America; and this, I believe, drove him beyond the limits of reason." Another reason for the rivalry between the brothers was that Edwin was perhaps the most famous actor of his day and John was struggling as an actor. A recent book by Nora Titone called *My Thoughts Be Bloody* asserts that this intense rivalry between brothers led the younger one to kill Abraham Lincoln.

The incident between Lincoln's son and his assassin's brother happened on a train platform in Jersey City, New Jersey. And although the exact date of the incident is not known, it probably took place in late 1863 or early 1864—in the midst of the Civil War. Robert Lincoln wrote of the incident in a letter to the editor of *The Century Magazine*: "The platform was about the height of the car floor, and there was of course a narrow space between the platform and the car body. There was some crowding, and I happened to be pressed by it against the car body while waiting my turn. In this situation the train began to move, and by the motion I was twisted off my feet, and had dropped somewhat, with feet downward, into the open space, and was personally helpless, when my coat collar was vigorously seized and I was quickly pulled up and out to a secure footing on the platform. Upon turning to thank my rescuer I saw it was Edwin Booth, whose face was of course well known to me, and I expressed my gratitude to him, and in doing so, called him by name."

Edwin Booth didn't know who he had saved that day until months later, when he received a letter from a friend who heard Robert Lincoln relate the story. It gave Edwin some comfort after the assassination, knowing he had saved the president's son, even as his brother took the president's life. After the assassination, Edwin retired from acting for about a year and worried that he would never be able to perform again. However, when he once again took to the stage, he received a prolonged standing ovation.

SIDE NOTE: Robert Todd Lincoln, the only one of Lincoln's children to survive into adulthood, seems a bit lost in the shadows of history due to his famous father. However, he was President James Garfield's secretary of war, minister to England under President Benjamin Harrison, and also president of the Pullman Car Company. The Republican Party even briefly considered him a potential presidential candidate.

RESOURCES

Beyer, Rick. *The Greatest War Stories Never Told: 100 Tales from Military History to Astonish, Bewilder & Stupefy.* New York: Harper Collins, 2005.

Browne, Ray B. and Kreiser, Jr., Lawrence A. *The Civil War and Reconstruction.* Westport, CT: Greenwood Press, 2003.

Boller, Jr., Paul F. *Not So!: Popular Myths About America from Columbus to Clinton.* New York: Oxford University Press, 1995.

Brinkley, Douglas. *The Wilderness Warrior: Theodore Roosevelt and the Crusade for America.* New York: Harper Collins, 2009.

Bruns, Roger. *Almost History: Close Calls, Plan B's, and Twists of Fate in America's Past.* New York: Hyperion, 2000.

Coren, Stanley. *The Pawprints of History.* New York: Free Press, 2003.

Crawfurd, Raymond. *Last Days of Charles II.* Oxford: Clarendon Press

Farquhar, Michael. *Treasury of Great American Scandals.* New York: Penguin Books, 2003.

Haught, James A. *Holy Horrors: An Illustrated History of Religious Murder and Madness.* New York: Prometheus Books, 1990.

Hughes, Lindsey. *Peter the Great: A Biography.* Bethany, CT: Yale University Press, 2002.

Leish, Kenneth (ed.). *The American Heritage Pictorial History of the Presidents of the United States.* New York: Simon & Schuster, 1989.

Long, Kim. *The Almanac of Political Corruption, Scandals, and Dirty Politics.* New York: Bantam Dell, 2007.

O'Connor, Jane. *If the Walls Could Talk: Family Life at the White House.* New York: Simon & Schuster, 2004.

Pearson, Will; Hattikudur, Mangesh; Hunt, Elizabeth, eds. *Mental Floss Presents: Forbidden Knowledge: A Wickedly Smart Guide to History's Naughtiest Bits.* New York: HarperCollins, 2005.

Poliakoff, Michael B. *Combat Sports in the Ancient World.* Bethany, CT: Yale University Press, 1987.

Powell, Michael. *Curious Events in History.* New York: Sterling Publishing Co., Inc., 2008.

Roberts II, John B. *Rating the First Ladies: The Women Who Influenced the Presidency.* New York: Citadel Press, 2003.

Sheinkin, Steve. *Two Miserable Presidents: Everything Your Schoolbooks Didn't Tell You About the Civil War.* New York: Roaring Brook Press, 2008.

St. George, Judith. *So You Want to Be President?* New York: Philomel Books, 2000.

Thornton, Brian. *The Book of Bastards: 101 Worst Scoundrels and Scandals from the World of Politics and Power.* Avon, MA: Adams Media, 2010.

Vennson, Anne Cipriano. *United States in the First World War: An Encyclopedia.* New York: Garland Reference Library of the Humanities, 1995.

INDEX